Can. Trust. Will.

Can. Trust. Will.

Hiring for the Human Element in the New Age of Cybersecurity

Leeza Garber and Scott Olson

BUSINESS EXPERT PRESS

Leader in applied, concise business books

Can. Trust. Will.:
Hiring for the Human Element in the New Age of Cybersecurity

Copyright © Business Expert Press, LLC, 2022.

Can. Trust. Will. is a Registered Trademark of Leeza Garber and Scott Olson

Cover design by Divya Pidaparti

Interior design by Exeter Premedia Services Private Ltd., Chennai, India

First published in 2022 by
Business Expert Press, LLC
222 East 46th Street, New York, NY 10017
www.businessexpertpress.com

ISBN-13: 978-1-63742-167-3 (paperback)
ISBN-13: 978-1-63742-168-0 (e-book)

Business Expert Press Business Law and Corporate Risk
Management Collection

Collection ISSN: 2333-6722 (print)
Collection ISSN: 2333-6730 (electronic)

First edition: 2022

10 9 8 7 6 5 4 3 2 1

Description

Cyber threats evolve at a staggering pace, and effective cybersecurity operations depend on successful teams. Unfortunately, statistics continue to illustrate that employers are not finding the people they need.

The Can. Trust. Will. system guides the C-Suite, human resources professionals, and talent acquisition to build unbeatable cybersecurity teams through advanced hiring processes and focused onboarding programs. Additionally, this book details how successful cybersecurity ecosystems are best built and sustained, with expert analysis from high-level government officials, Fortune 500 CSOs and CISOs, risk managers, and even a few techies.

Those already in the field (and newbies) will glean invaluable knowledge about how to find their most effective position within a cybersecurity ecosystem. In a tech-driven environment, cybersecurity is fundamentally a human problem: and the first step is to hire for the human element.

Keywords

cybersecurity; human resources; information technology; data breach; hiring; c-suite; onboarding; interview; career; behavioral interview; budget; budget process; security budget; IT; talent acquisition

Contents

Preface ix

Introduction xv

Chapter 1   Identifying Your Cybersecurity Hiring Need 1

Chapter 2   Can–Trust–Will 25

Chapter 3   Finding the Right Candidates 57

Chapter 4   The Big Mistake (and How to Avoid It) 85

Chapter 5   Hiring the Right Cybersecurity Role Behaviors 105

Chapter 6   The Interview 131

Chapter 7   Onboarding Cybersecurity Hires (and Building
             Cybersecurity Into Onboarding) 157

Chapter 8   Concluding Thoughts and Tips for Candidates 177

Appendix A: Model Behavioral Question Sets 183

Appendix B: Additional Behavioral Question Sets 191

About the Authors 195

Index 197

Preface

Why We Chose to Write This Book

From humble beginnings of the Arpanet and a worm called "Creeper," cybersecurity as a field has grown by leaps and bounds. Now, in the year 2022, every private corporation, government entity, public school, private university, mom-and-pop shop, massive financial institution, and local bank branch must consider cybersecurity and the people they hire to carry out cybersecurity directives. The massive growth of the field is staggering, with demand for cybersecurity experts estimated to be growing twelve times faster than the current job market in the United States.[1] In short, every industry is struggling to find and retain employees that address cybersecurity needs. The structured solution offered in this book will guide the C-Suite, internal and external talent acquisition teams, and human resource professionals charged with navigating this challenging arena. Eligible employees come from information technology, engineering, security, privacy, risk, legal, computing, and human resources backgrounds, each offering a different piece of the puzzle. Compounding the complexity of the concept we term "cybersecurity" is the variety of full-time, part-time, contract, and "As A Service" ("AAS") employees every employer must consider. What we have found, over and over again, is that cybersecurity is fundamentally a human problem—and must be addressed accordingly.

We have been fortunate enough to speak with leaders in this space from a wide range of backgrounds, and have incorporated their valuable insight into our hiring model. From the Director of the National Initiative for Cybersecurity Education at the National Institute of Standards and Technology in the U.S. Department of Commerce; to the Director of Information Security Governance Risk and Compliance for

---

[1] National Initiative for Cybersecurity Careers and Studies, *Veterans: Launch a New Cybersecurity Career*. https://niccs.us-cert.gov/training/veterans

the University of Wisconsin System; to the Vice President and Chief Security Officer of Dominion Energy (a major energy supplier for the U.S. government and countless private entities); to the former Chief Information Officer of the U.S. Air Force and current Senior Vice President of Leidos (the largest IT provider in the federal market); to the Director of Technology Infrastructure and Information Security of a Major League Baseball Team.

Outline

Technology is inherently and firmly rooted in everyday life. Safe interaction with information technology systems is increasingly important. Fortunately, many companies are aware of the risk and corresponding liability which arise from maintaining ever-growing amounts of data, and they emphasize building systems which will stay ahead of cyber threat vectors. Developing and implementing solutions to ongoing cyberattacks and data breaches requires creative, focused, and highly trained employees. The challenge is finding the right people who are capable of creating effective solutions to evolving problems. As a result, the cyber world is struggling to find the human capital it needs.

It was predicted that there would be 3.5 million unfilled cybersecurity jobs globally by 2021, up from one million positions in 2014.[2] Unfortunately, the cybersecurity workforce gap continues to increase: as of 2019, it was estimated that the U.S. cybersecurity workforce needed to grow by sixty-two percent in order to meet nationwide demand.[3]

Compounding this problem is the fact that clear descriptions of job roles and responsibilities are substantially lacking. The research shows that professionals in the field of cybersecurity respond better to clearly defined job requirements and descriptions. Vague descriptions are not only a

---

[2] Cybersecurity Ventures, *Cybersecurity Talent Crunch to Create 3.5 Million Unfilled Jobs Globally by 2021.* https://cybersecurityventures.com/jobs/

[3] (ISC)², *Cybersecurity Workforce Study 2019.* www.isc2.org/-/media/ISC2/Research/2019-Cybersecurity-Workforce-Study/ISC2-Cybersecurity-Workforce-Study-2019.ashx (3)

"turn-off" to those with experience but also create confusion for newbies.[4] When non-manager level cybersecurity professionals were asked "What about a job description demonstrates an employer's lack of cybersecurity knowledge?" seventy percent respondents replied it was when the description was "too vague," and forty-eight percent of executive management concurred.[5] A runner-up problem was when the job description "didn't accurately reflect the position details or responsibilities."[6]

Defining who you need for certain roles is more challenging for jobs relating to cybersecurity because these positions are situated in a rapidly evolving field involving specialized skills which must be adapted to unique workplace environments. Even though the initial strategy at the outset is often to set the bar high, begin reviewing applicants, and then compromise on one or a few competencies, this compromise is rarely realized. This is because once a "good enough" candidate is identified, at least one person in the approval pipeline will ask why a candidate who fails to meet the job description is being considered at all. But there are valuable cybersecurity candidates—whether for technical, compliance, risk, legal, or executive roles—that come from all different backgrounds and can be trained. The real question is: do you know (and understand) what you need?

The single most important part of this process is often overlooked by most hiring professionals, and not only those focused on cybersecurity. To hire effectively, you must know, in specific detail, exactly who and what you need for each specific position. Job competencies, particularly those based on surveys or industry research, are insufficient because they are too general. Relying on credentials or completion of specific training courses, without a deeper dive, is also not enough to differentiate between candidates who will succeed and those who will fail. Defining who you need for certain roles is more challenging for jobs relating to cybersecurity because these positions present a field that involves specialized skills

---

[4] (ISC)², *Hiring and Retaining Top Cybersecurity Talent.* www.isc2.org/-/media/Files/Research/ISC2-Hiring-and-Retaining-Top-Cybersecurity-Talent.ashx (10)

[5] *Id.*

[6] *Id.*

which must be adapted to unique workplace environments. Paul Maurer,[7] the president of Montreat College (which is a National Center of Academic Excellence in Cyber Defense Education), explains why cybersecurity is a human problem:

> **Paul Maurer:** Here's the basic value proposition that we came to after a year of market-testing, in boardrooms, in Washington D.C., in partnership with a think tank in D.C.: that cybersecurity is not principally a technical problem. The problem of cybersecurity is principally a human problem. Therefore, the solution to cybersecurity is not principally a technical solution. It is principally a human solution. If you don't have people with the right character and ethics as your cyber leaders, as your cyber operators, your technology doesn't matter very much. We don't think that AI alone can solve the cyber problem. We think humans principally need to solve the cyber problem.[8]

The first section of this book dives into the particulars of cybersecurity—the laws, regulatory bodies, and careers that impact and influence hiring needs, obligations, and budgets.

Afterward, we describe our proprietary hiring model that best applies to cybersecurity workforce development. In reviewing how to use this model, we offer solutions for defining and assembling the right candidate pool, how to use a resumé most efficiently, and how to develop a candidate description and corresponding question sets that will facilitate the extraction of relevant data. The goal is to make better hiring decisions. We will address common pitfalls and how to avoid them; in particular, the

---

[7] Paul Maurer serves as president of Montreat College in North Carolina. Montreat College is a National Center of Academic Excellence in Cyber Defense Education as designated by the NSA and DHS. The college offers four levels of cyber education: certificate programs, Associate of Applied Science in Cybersecurity, Bachelor of Science in Cybersecurity, and MBA with a concentration in cybersecurity management. Montreat emphasizes the role of character and ethics as central to being trusted cyber leaders and professionals.

[8] P. Maurer, in discussion with the authors. July 13, 2020.

concepts of "fit", "a great addition to the team," and "taking a chance" as bases for hiring decisions will be analyzed, and processes for how to avoid them given in detail.

With a comprehensive analysis of the current cybersecurity workforce, backed by in-depth interviews with leading industry experts, statistics from government and the private sector, and data breach stories pulled directly from the headlines, this book serves as a practical guide to adeptly find, differentiate, and hire the appropriate and necessary cybersecurity workforce. It is the most effective way to face the cutting-edge nature of cybersecurity in the first half of the twenty-first century.

Introduction

The Equifax Teachable Moment

The story of the Equifax breach is the nightmare wake-up call that every organization dreads. The high-level overview is simple: Equifax, a major consumer reporting agency, failed to properly address a critical Apache Struts software vulnerability. Arguably, the most important, intriguing, and insidious detail lies at the root cause of the breach, however. When you dig a little further into the weeds, and look past the inadequate security program, the outlier Internet-facing 1970s legacy operating system using Apache Struts, the lacking communication chain, and dysfunctional oversight, this massive data breach was actually a people problem.

Based on the sordid backstory provided by the House Oversight Report, and tech blogs, the real heart of Equifax's misfortune stemmed from . . . a hiring issue. Equifax's history shows that back in 2005, the CIO and then newly hired CSO did not get along due to "fundamental disagreements," and the decision was made to "move the security function out of IT and into the legal office."[1] Upon this change, the Chief Legal Officer was thereafter referred to as the "head of security," and Equifax continued with its goal of establishing its first companywide IT security standards.[2] However, in 2010, the CIO was replaced and then in 2013 so was the CSO. Still, the siloed reporting structure stayed the same (though not without employees questioning it).

> The functional result of the CIO/CSO structure meant IT operational and security responsibilities were split, creating an accountability gap. At the time of the breach, Equifax's-

---

[1] U.S. House of Representatives Committee on Oversight and Government Reform, *The Equifax Data Breach*. 115th Congress. https://republicans-oversight. house.gov/wp-content/uploads/2018/12/Equifax-Report.pdf (55)

[2] *Id.* at 55–56.

organizational structure did not facilitate a strong CIO and CSO partnership. Testimony demonstrated the disconnect between IT operations and security.[3]

The "fundamental disagreements" that haunted the relationship between the CIO and CSO had a major ripple effect on Equifax's structure, security, and solidity, and arguably helped set the stage for the perfect storm in the 2017 data breach.

It is not unusual for businesses and government entities to have teams that include people that do not get along. However, it is unusual for such teams to succeed.

Cybersecurity leaders must have a seat at the table to create, develop, and sustain a meaningful cybersecurity program throughout an organization. Such a program relies on the cybersecurity culture of the workplace.

Cybersecurity Culture in the Workplace

Cybersecurity culture, in any organization, requires everyone to take part in some way. This is most obvious in the C-Suite (as illustrated by Equifax's misfortune). Every part of the C-Suite alphabet soup must integrate cybersecurity into company culture through example, strategic decision making, and leadership.

Hiring for cybersecurity and cybersecurity-related positions is made difficult by a relatively small talent pool, high demand, and by the significant nature of the tasks assigned. There is no doubt that in an exploding field, cybersecurity talent is more difficult to find.[4] "Today's skilled cybersecurity professionals are in high demand," with no signs of slowing.[5] Furthermore, as illustrated by the U.S. Bureau of Labor Statistics, "[e]mployment of information security analysts is projected to grow thirty-two percent from 2018 to 2028, much faster than the average for all

---

[3] *Id.* at 58.

[4] ISACA, *State of Cybersecurity 2019, Part 1: Current Trends in Workforce Development.* www.isaca.org/bookstore/state-of-cybersecurity-2019/whpsc191 (18)

[5] *Id.*

occupations. Demand for information security analysts is expected to be very high, as these analysts will be needed to create innovative solutions to prevent hackers from stealing critical information or causing problems for computer networks."[6]

Creating and maintaining a culture of cybersecurity in the workplace is no easy task. As Adam Lee,[7] the Vice President and Chief Security Officer of Dominion Energy, explains:

> **Adam:** Dominion Energy is a highly disciplined, core values-led company. It rightly perceives itself as a critical national asset and its culture has formed around that notion. The overall enterprise security culture is strong. My organization, Corporate Intelligence and Security, is regarded by many in government, in the sector, and in the trade groups as a best practice; I think Dominion's leaders are proud of what the company has built. That said, it took ten to fifteen years of effort to achieve with slow, often painful gains at the start.[8]

Spotlight: Working From Home

The COVID-19 outbreak forced many businesses' hands regarding cybersecurity preparedness. Throughout the world, employees (who were fortunate enough to be able to) immediately began working from home. There are certain jobs that are impossible to translate to a home environment. However, those that began to set up shop from their home offices, couches, and kitchen tables were not only confronted with the distractions of spouses, partners, kids, pets, and everything else but were also

---

[6] Bureau of Labor Statistics, U.S. Department of Labor, *Occupational Outlook Handbook: Information Security Analysts.* www.bls.gov/ooh/computer-and-information-technology/information-security-analysts.htm

[7] Adam Lee was the special agent in charge of the FBI's Richmond Division before joining Dominion Energy, where he currently is responsible for physical and cybersecurity across the entirety of the organization.

[8] A. Lee, in discussion with the authors. July 09, 2020.

confronting massive increases in cybersecurity threats and (for some) a corresponding lack of guidance, proactivity, and preparedness.

Ongoing cybersecurity awareness and related training is always important, but the pandemic amplified its significance. And employees handling cybersecurity had to pivot quickly to address new concerns. Andrea Markstrom,[9] the Chief Information Officer of Taft Stettinius & Hollister LLP and 2019 NYC CIO of the Year award winner,[10] attempted to find a silver lining in the midst of crisis, by keeping security awareness top of mind:

> **Andrea:** One of the pieces that is always at the forefront of my mind is the ongoing security awareness that is needed. I'll take every opportunity that I can to provide awareness. For example, we've got the formal security awareness training in place, but with coronavirus, we pivoted everybody to work from home, for a while it was daily, then it was weekly, but it was how to protect the firm and client data. How to protect your home. Reminders. You're going to get phishing emails—the phishing attempts went through the roof. So every opportunity that I can to provide and speak up about security awareness I will do so.[11]

Statistics are still becoming available, and later on, hindsight will be 20/20. But a Gallup poll dated March 30 through April 2, 2020, which tracked how the U.S. workforce is dealing with COVID-19-related disruptions to their jobs, found that sixty-two percent of employed Americans are working from home (a number that has doubled from mid-March). Also significant, three in five of those polled, who were working from home due to the pandemic, would "prefer to continue to work remotely as much as possible, once public health restrictions are

---

[9] Andrea Markstrom is the CIO of Taft Stettinius & Hollister LLP, where she is responsible for firm-wide information technology and security initiatives across all of Taft's offices and practices areas. She has more than twenty-five years of experience as a recognized leader in the field.

[10] From the CIO Inspire Leadership Organization.

[11] A. Markstrom, in discussion with the authors. June 24, 2020.

lifted."[12] Another survey found that, of 550 respondents between March 12 and March 16, two-thirds noted that the shift to work from home involved "employees who do not typically work remotely."[13]

Gail Gottehrer,[14] a renowned emerging technologies lawyer, pointed out that this exact shift—from employees who don't typically work remotely to a sudden forced work-from-home environment—was especially difficult for many law firms (though her analysis can be analogized to other public and private entities that struggle with technology and cybersecurity in general):

> **Gail:** Lately, I get asked about law firm cybersecurity during the pandemic. You could have had a great plan for law firm cybersecurity, but unless you predicted the pandemic, you were probably not anticipating the way that most law firms' lawyers are working now. If somebody had said a year ago that you're going to be communicating with a court through Zoom, you would have said they were crazy. But that's the world we live in now, and it's going to be for the foreseeable future. So the critical skill is being able to say, "Yes, the plan I devised and put into effect in January was great for January, but the world now, since March, is completely different and changing by the day, so I need to adapt and create a new plan."[15]

An intriguing example of how cybersecurity culture is forcibly changing in the wake of the pandemic is how attorneys (and most certainly

---

[12] B. Megan. *U.S. Workers Discovering Affinity for Remote Work.* Gallup. https://news.gallup.com/poll/306695/workers-discovering-affinity-remote-work.aspx

[13] D. Wiessner. *Remote work is new territory for many employers—Seyfarth Shaw survey.* Reuters. www.reuters.com/article/employment-seyfarth/in-brief-remote-work-is-new-territory-for-many-employers-seyfarth-shaw-survey-idUSL1N2B-C29J

[14] After practicing law at law firms for over twenty years, Gail recently founded her own firm, where her practice focuses on emerging technologies-related litigation and counseling, including autonomous vehicle regulation, drones, artificial intelligence, biometrics, data privacy, and cybersecurity.

[15] G. Gottehrer, in discussion with the authors. July 09, 2020.

other employees with access to private data) must be aware of smart devices potentially recording their attorney–client privileged conversations. Importantly, the Pennsylvania Bar Association actually released a formal ethics opinion in April 2020 on the subject, entitled, "Prohibiting the use of smart devices such as those offered by Amazon Alexa and Google voice assistants in locations where client-related conversations may occur."[16] These seemingly small technical pieces all make up part of the larger work-from-home puzzle, which requires cybersecurity expertise from all angles.

Send-Off Thoughts Before Beginning of Book

The strategies outlined in this book create foundational pillars for addressing cybersecurity hiring. By breaking down and clarifying the fundamental issues inherent in understanding what type of cybersecurity needs must be addressed (beginning with writing a job description that covers all facets of the right fit, why behavioral analysis is vital to successful cybersecurity hiring, and illuminating the concept of "shared intention" in corporate cybersecurity culture), best practices in analyzing and acting upon cybersecurity hires will be explained, discussed, and reinforced through the use of real-life examples and situational analysis. The reader will be able to develop a foundational knowledge base and skill set in order to succeed in finding and hiring the optimal cybersecurity team members.

---

[16] Pennsylvania Bar Association, *Best Practices When Performing Legal Work and Communications Remotely: General Considerations.* www.pabar.org/members/catalogs/Ethics%20Opinions/formal/F2020-300.pdf (8)

CHAPTER 1

Identifying Your Cybersecurity Hiring Need

In order to hire cybersecurity-related employees, or outsource the cybersecurity work, the hiring entities must understand and appreciate how cybersecurity issues impact their business.

Knowing What You Don't Know

The wisdom of our own ignorance is invaluable. Cybersecurity may appear as an illusory concept to many, especially those who do not interact with the field on a daily basis. In today's climate, however, it is impossible to be in the C-Suite and/or in a position evaluating new hires without at least superficially understanding and addressing the who/what/when/where/why/how of cybersecurity interaction within your workplace. Inherent in that understanding is appreciating what we do not know: What laws apply? What obligations do we have to our clients? What obligations do we have to our employees? What cyber risk do we face?

Any cybersecurity hiring program should begin with an assessment of what current, filled roles touch on cybersecurity and address follow-up questions on success and satisfaction. Certainly, some current employees should and will already be tackling cybersecurity tasks (even if it's just to outsource them to outside counsel, consultants, and/or vendors). An audit of these positions is imperative to establish foundational knowledge. Gail answers the basic question of why we need to care:

Gail: I think the challenge is, first of all, to make companies recognize that everybody is a target. Certain clients say, "Look, I'm not IBM, I'm not Pfizer, I don't have medical information, I'm not a billion-dollar company, I'm not on the Forbes 100 list—no one's interested in hacking my company." I tell them, even if you're the corner ice cream store you have valuable data and are at risk. If you have an employee, you have social security information and medical information about that employee; if you're a slightly larger company and you're covered by federal laws, you have requests for medical leave and payroll information. No matter who you are, whatever data you have has value to somebody, and it's a low cost investment for them to try to get it, and that's the reality we need to be prepared to address.[1]

In order to know what we don't know, we have to help each other. For most entities, this means opening up continuous and constructive dialogue across internal lines—legal, finance, information technology, human resources, administration, and operations—to acknowledge and appreciate where the gaps are. Unfortunately, some cybersecurity departments (whether due to outside stereotypes or actual practices) are known as the folks that create new impediments (instituting secure authentication measures) and require increased review of new practices (blocking that cool new tech gadget). But as Michael Woodson,[2] the Director of Information Security and Privacy for Sonesta, points out, this shouldn't be how the department is viewed:

Michael: We're not in the business of "no," we're in the business of "right." The relationship that you have with the business unit is to tell them that you want to do the right thing; that you're meeting the standards; that you're putting the right security controls in, so that you're in compliance where it is required. But also at the end

---

[1] G. Gottehrer, in discussion with the authors. July 09, 2020.

[2] Michael Woodson was with the Boston Police Department and consulted for the U.S. Department of Justice and Department of State for many years before becoming the Director of Cyber and Network Security at Santander Bank, and then moving to the CISO role at the Massachusetts Bay Transportation Authority. He is currently the Director of Information Security and Privacy for Sonesta.

of the day, we want to make sure we're providing good advice on how to put something in, in a secure way.[3]

Michael's modus operandi, that his department is not in the business of "no" but in the business of "right," is the way cybersecurity teams should be viewed. Current ways of doing business, for almost every entity, require a solid appreciation and acceptance for how cybersecurity fits into all operations. Whether it is a cybersecurity department, small team, or two-person show, this aspect of the organization should be viewed as a benefit, as a business value-add in so many ways.

But cybersecurity teams have to prove themselves; this is a common theme. Adam Lee describes the "growing pains" in creating a solid cybersecurity culture:

> **Adam:** [Creating cybersecurity culture] took top leadership agreeing to what, at the time, were very hard decisions—such as taking away network admin rights, not allowing random, personally-owned USB drives, requiring annual training by one-hundred percent of employees, paying for the required cyber defenses year over year, hiring dedicated staff to perform those functions and growing that over time, being willing to set aside the complaints about "hurting my productivity" realizing that without a rock-solid cyber defense there would be zero productivity if ransomware ripped through the organization, and more. Those are hard things to do when starting out. The voices of dissent are loud. The costs are large. The impact can be tangible and felt—not always in what is perceived a good way but is, in the end, critical.[4]

Adam gets into the nitty gritty of what cybersecurity covers, including the frustrations associated with basic technical issues (like access rights and policies surrounding external drives), to the larger, more amorphous aspects like productivity, budget, and the critical nature of the beast.

---

[3] M. Woodson, in discussion with the authors. July 20, 2020.
[4] A. Lee, in discussion with the authors. July 09, 2020.

Cybersecurity Obligations

The obligations surrounding cybersecurity are frustratingly cutting edge. The body of guidance from state, federal, and supreme courts, in addition to Federal Trade Commission actions and settlements, is constantly growing and requires attention.

> **Gail:** I tell my clients that you have to embrace cybersecurity, that there are so many laws now, it's getting to be a public expectation. If you have to do it anyway and you don't want to risk the liability, you should make it something positive—tell your customers and potential customers that you take their privacy seriously. Tell them, "We care about your data, we understand that when we collect your biometric data, it's your iris scan and it's your child's iris scan—it's something personal to you that can't be changed. And we're going to go above and beyond what the law requires, and take even more cybersecurity precautions than anybody else in the industry, and that's why you should do business with us and not the competition."[5]

There is no substitute for consulting in-house or outside counsel regarding legal cybersecurity responsibilities (and this book does not claim to, nor does it, provide legal advice). Still, it is important for every head of division to be aware of what obligations may exist, and how state and federal laws are evolving. A recent heavy-hitter state law, which sprang into effect in January 2020, is California's Consumer Privacy Act (CCPA). Building off of the European Union's General Data Protection Regulation (GDPR), the CCPA proactively "… grants California consumers robust data privacy rights and control over their personal information, including the right to know, the right to delete, and the right to opt-out of the sale of personal information that businesses collect, as well as additional protections for minors."[6] This inherently requires dutiful

---

[5] G. Gottehrer, in discussion with the authors. July 09, 2020.

[6] State of California Department of Justice, *California Consumer Privacy Act*. https://oag.ca.gov/privacy/ccpa

attention to how corporations handle these obligations, on legal and technical scales. Amanda Tilley,[7] the Vice President of Information Security Management for OceanFirst Bank, explained the significance of privacy laws for cybersecurity professionals:

> **Amanda:** Over the past decade, I've seen a shift in how privacy laws have become more of a concern for cybersecurity professionals. As cybersecurity professionals, our job is to protect the confidentiality, integrity, and availability of information. To do this effectively, we must know where our data lives. Knowing what data is where is imperative to complying with consumer privacy laws, from breach notification requirements to a consumer's right to know or right to be forgotten. Not understanding consumer privacy laws within applicable jurisdictions can result in fines, penalties, and damage to an organization's reputation. While NIST, CSF and GLBA are foundational for cybersecurity in banking, we are still beholden to, as Leeza would say, "the patchwork of privacy laws of the United States."[8]

The patchwork shows no signs of going away, despite presidential promises and congressional press releases. New York answered with the Stop Hacks and Improve Electronic Data Security (SHIELD) Act, which fully came into effect in March 2020. In its quest to amend and update the state's 2005 data breach law, the SHIELD Act broadened the scope of data covered under the notification law, updated the notification requirements after a breach, and broadened the definition of a data breach—in essence, the Act greatly increased the tasks and liability organizations face

---

[7] Amanda Tilley is the Vice President of Information Security Management Governance, Risk, Compliance and Privacy for OceanFirst Bank. She is a certified Project Management Professional (PMP®) and Associate Business Continuity Professional (ABCP®). She is currently pursuing a master's degree in Legal Studies with concentrations in Cybersecurity and Information Privacy Law and Financial Regulatory Compliance from Drexel University's Kline School of Law. (She was also a student in Leeza's Information Privacy Law class.)

[8] A. Tilley, in discussion with the authors. July 02, 2020.

on the cybersecurity front.[9] As the Society for Human Resource Management (SHRM) points out, the breadth of the SHIELD Act means HR stakeholders (arguably, this could also include cybersecurity stakeholders) must address the necessity of designating (or hiring) an employee to coordinate the data security program, training employees in a best security practices program, and choosing relevant service providers, as necessary.[10]

Some of the state laws are even more specific; in early 2017, the New York Department of Financial Services imposed stricter cybersecurity regulations in the form of 23 NYCRR 500: Cybersecurity Requirements for Financial Services Companies. This update requires that all covered entities "... designate a qualified individual responsible for overseeing and implementing the Covered Entity's cybersecurity program and enforcing its cybersecurity policy (for purposes of this Part, 'Chief Information Security Officer' [CISO]). The CISO may be employed by the Covered Entity, one of its Affiliates or a Third Party Service Provider." [Section 500.04(a)] And further, "The CISO of each Covered Entity shall report in writing at least annually to the Covered Entity's board of directors or equivalent governing body. If no such board of directors or equivalent governing body exists, such report shall be timely presented to a Senior Officer of the Covered Entity responsible for the Covered Entity's cybersecurity program." [Section 500.04 (b)] In one fell swoop, this regulation necessitated the roles of a CISO and potentially a senior officer responsible for the "cybersecurity program." Other states are following suit, with many legislative proposals being considered as of the writing on this book.

As of early 2020, the Pentagon is also beginning to phase in a new cybersecurity standards schema that hopeful vendors must comply with—including critical security requirements. The Cybersecurity Maturity Model Certification Model Version 1.0 (CMMC), which is set to be realized over the next five years or so, adds "... a certification element to verify the implementation of processes and practices associated with the

---

[9] Senate Bill S5575B, 2019–2020 Legislative Session. www.nysenate.gov/legislation/bills/2019/s5575

[10] P. Gordon and T. Jennifer. August 28, 2019. "The New York Shield Act: What Employers Need to Know." www.pages/new-york-shield-act.aspx

achievement of a cybersecurity maturity level."[11] This new set of obligations will warrant attention from many businesses' hiring teams.

Beyond legal obligations, clients and consumers may have a separate layer of requests. There are a variety of nationally and internationally accepted (and requested) standards: the National Institute of Standards and Technology (NIST) Cybersecurity Framework, the International Organization for Standardization (ISO) Information Technology and Information Security Management Systems 27001 Standard Series, and the Payment Card Industry Data Security Standard (PCI DSS). While not necessarily legally mandatory (depending on industry and partner and/or vendor agreements), these "best practices" are often requested by knowledgeable clients. Adam has created a custom program:

> **Adam:** I base our program on what works the best from ALL the frameworks I can consume. None are perfect. None are complete. None are actually prescriptive roadmaps. All require subjective interpretation. Frameworks are simply guidelines of good practices. They are menus of things that are all "healthy and good for you"—a framework may tell you to eat spinach, but [you] would be fine eating another healthy option instead. My point is, build your criteria from many sources and find what works in your culture, what words resonate with your leadership, and what model is easiest for you to consume, measure, fund, and achieve results. Dominion Energy's framework is bespoke and built from pieces and parts of them all.[12]

Many companies function with bespoke frameworks—it depends on the corporate culture, legal obligations, consumer awareness, and industry.

Finally, almost any type of vendor that has computer- and Internet-based capabilities may find that clients (and potential clients) may want proof of a cybersecurity and/or technological audit. These audits may be termed "cybersecurity compliance audits," "cybersecurity assessments,"

---

[11] Cybersecurity Model Maturity Certification, Version 1.0. (January 30, 2020). www.acq.osd.mil/cmmc/docs/CMMC_Model_Main_20200203.pdf (2)

[12] A. Lee, in discussion with the authors. July 09, 2020.

"IT security audits," and so on (the iterations are limitless); the common theme is that, well, someone (more likely, some team) has to do it. And update it annually, if not more frequently.

Alphabet Soup of Cybersecurity Roles

The field of cybersecurity is, definitively, an alphabet soup.

> From governmental entities (including but not limited to Cybersecurity and Infrastructure Security Agency [CISA], Cyberspace Solarium Commission [CSC], Office of Cybersecurity, Energy Security, and Emergency Response [CESER]);

> To federal regulation (including but not limited to the Health Insurance Portability and Accountability Act [HIPAA], Gramm-Leach-Bliley Act [GLBA]);

> To state bodies (including but not limited to the New York State Chief Information Security Office [NYS CISO], the California Cybersecurity Integration Center [CCIC], Texas Office of the Chief Information Security Officer [OCISO], Massachusetts Executive Office of Technology Services and Security [EOTSS]);

> To employee titles (Chief Information Officer [CIO], Chief Technology Officer [CTO], Chief Security Officer [CSO], CISO, Information Technology [IT], Chief Privacy Officer [CPO]), we cover every letter of the alphabet in triplicate. And new offices, agencies, laws, and titles are emerging every day.

Spotlight: NIST and NICE

The NIST National Initiative for Cybersecurity Education Cybersecurity Workforce Framework, known as the NICE Framework, defines a spectrum of cybersecurity roles described through knowledge, skills, and abilities in detail, offering a government standard against which to compare.[13]

---

[13] NIST Special Publication 800–181: National Initiative for Cybersecurity Education (NICE) Cybersecurity Workforce Framework. https://nvlpubs.nist.gov/nistpubs/SpecialPublications/NIST.SP.800-181.pdf (NICE Cybersecurity Workforce Framework).

However, it is important to point out that each of the cybersecurity-specific job responsibilities can vary widely depending on organization size, industry, setup, and mission. The NICE Framework explains that its extensive catalog can be used as a "nonprescriptive cybersecurity workforce dictionary," which can lead to better communication surrounding "recruiting, retention, and training."[14]

Importantly, the NIST Framework for Improving Critical Infrastructure Cybersecurity does specify personnel in various core functions, including "Identify: Asset Management" (regarding mapping organizational communication and establishing cybersecurity roles and responsibilities for the entire workforce), "Protect: Awareness and Training" (further development of the discussion of roles and responsibilities and privilege), "Protect: Information Protection Processes and Procedures" (cybersecurity is included in HR practices, including personnel screening), and "Respond: Communications" (when a response is necessary, personnel know their roles and order of operations, coordination with stakeholders).[15] The NICE Framework, however, provides a granular database focused solely on cybersecurity workforce personnel.

The NICE Framework is broken down into seven major categories, which are further broken down into thirty-three subcategories, and then the tertiary layer is the specific work roles (defined by their correlating tasks, knowledge, skills, and abilities). Tasks (i.e., "T0043: Coordinate with enterprise-wide cyber defense staff to validate network alerts"), knowledge (i.e., "K0193: Knowledge of advanced data remediation security features in databases"), skills (i.e., "S0299: Skill in wireless network target analysis, templating, and geolocation"), and abilities (i.e., "A0082: Ability to effectively collaborate via virtual teams") are listed by the hundreds, identifying smaller puzzle pieces that come together to create each of the work roles, as NICE has defined them.[16] It is a hefty framework, and deserves recognition. While we acknowledge and appreciate the exquisite level of detail and finely tuned organization, it still can be overwhelming to private companies. Michael Woodson explains his perspective on the NICE Framework:

---

[14] *Id.* at 2–3.

[15] NIST. *Framework for Improving Critical Infrastructure Cybersecurity, Version 1.1.* https://nvlpubs.nist.gov/nistpubs/CSWP/NIST.CSWP.04162018.pdf (24–41).

[16] *NICE Cybersecurity Workforce Framework*, Appendices A.4–A.7.

Michael: The NICE Framework is nice to do, but it may not be a reality, because the reality of your organization may not be mature enough for it. I'm not seeing a lot of people being able to do that, to do it properly. In my world, that wouldn't work. For a global company, that could work. It locks you into a certain way of doing things in your business. And some people don't like it—they want to be agile. The components are—to me—more focused towards government, not necessarily towards business.[17]

Still, NICE continues to work to help raise awareness about implementation strategies. In essence, the NICE Framework should at the very least be a reference point for businesses in the process of creating, organizing, or rebooting their cyber units. In fact, General Bill Bender,[18] the former CIO of the United States Air Force and current Senior Vice President at Leidos (a Fortune 500 science and technology company), explains how Leidos has adapted the NICE Framework—and even further amplified it:

Bill: At Leidos, our cyber workforce numbers around 1,300, and that includes those who would be primarily focused on the business itself: protecting our systems and keeping a large defense contractor up and operating and safe and secure, but also a whole host of subject matter experts that are helping build better solutions that we implement for the government under contract. So their approach is very much in keeping with the NICE Framework, but pretty much on steroids. And in some cases, it could be argued that we have taken it further than even NICE maybe envisioned it or at least others, both commercially and certainly in government, have advanced. There are twenty-seven different work roles

---

[17] M. Woodson, in discussion with the authors. July 20, 2020.
[18] General Bill Bender is the former Chief Information Officer of the United States Air Force, where he led three directorates and supported 54,000 cyber operations and support personnel across the globe with a portfolio valued at $17 billion. As of Fall 2017, General Bender became the Senior Vice President of Strategic Accounts and Government Relations at Leidos, where he brings his thirty-four years of military experience to the strategic role.

associated with our cyber workforce, five or six sub-families of those roles, and all of the sundry field aptitudes and experiences, broken down to an atomic level in terms of what the proficiency is required in order to attain that role and to be considered proficient to various levels.[19]

However, we do note that the NICE Framework does not cover the significance of behavioral characteristics. While the "abilities" portion references the ability to coordinate with senior leadership, the ability to collaborate, the ability to think critically, and A0067: "[a]bility to adjust to and operate in a diverse, unpredictable, challenging, and fast-paced work environment," there seems to be a presumption that if a person has the ability to do these things then they necessarily will do them, particularly when under stress. We differentiate between the "ability," which is a measure of whether a person can execute the described behavior, and "behavioral characteristic," which is a measure of the likelihood that the person actually will execute the described behavior when called upon to do so.

In organizations that have 500 or more employees, studies have found that sixty-two percent of their cybersecurity teams are led by a CISO, while twenty-seven percent are led by a senior IT executive.[20] In smaller companies' cybersecurity units, it appears that fifty percent are led by a CISO and thirty percent are led by a senior IT executive.[21] Regardless of what title is used, "cybersecurity" roles can be the obvious heavy hitters, like the CISO, CSO, IT lead, or security architects—but they can also be (and typically include) the lawyers, risk management, project managers, operations employees, and many others. It is vital to understand what job functions you need fulfilled, describe them specifically, describe the relevant and necessary behaviors, and name the role accordingly. Rodney

---

[19] B. Bender, in discussion with the authors. July 08, 2020.

[20] (ISC)², Strategies for Building and Growing Strong Cybersecurity Teams, (ISC)² Workforce Study, 2019. www.isc2.org/-/media/ISC2/Research/2019-Cybersecurity-Workforce-Study/ISC2-Cybersecurity-Workforce-Study-2019.ashx (17)

[21] *Id.*

Petersen, the director of NICE,[22] explains why a narrow interpretation of what cybersecurity is hinders workforce development:

> **Rodney:** I want us to think about the breadth of things that are impacted by cybersecurity work. That's what the NICE Framework is trying to address. It's not just the cybersecurity workforce. One of the things we're proposing changing is the name of the NICE Framework, which may seem a subtle thing, but a cybersecurity workforce framework tends to be interpreted narrowly as if it's just the people who work in the cybersecurity organization or for the CISO or those who perform work roles in the "protect and defend" category. We're renaming the NICE Framework as the NICE Workforce Framework for Cybersecurity; to be about the workforce for cybersecurity, to keep the focus broader than the people who have cybersecurity in their title—or are part of the cybersecurity organization. Instead, we want organizations to really think more broadly about the people who directly impact cybersecurity.[23]

Rodney's insightful commentary hits home on so many levels of the thought process involved in cybersecurity roles. Regardless of whether the term "cybersecurity" appears in the title or not, a large cross-section of employees in any given business will need to address cybersecurity tasks, whatever those might be.

A few more letters to add to the titular and abbreviations mix are "AAS"—"As A Service." The AAS, or outsourced, cybersecurity employee model can be a good fit for certain companies, smaller nonprofits, and boutique businesses. The AAS can be a contract to hire, full-time, part-time, or consultant roles. These vendors can range from outside cybersecurity counsel, to managed security operations centers (SOCs), to as-needed penetration testers, to antivirus implementation specialists,

---

[22] Rodney Petersen is the director of the National Initiative for Cybersecurity Education (NICE) at the National Institute of Standards and Technology (NIST) in the U.S. Department of Commerce.

[23] R. Petersen, in discussion with the authors. July 28, 2020.

to security training, to on-demand incident response teams. Almost any cybersecurity service can be an AAS, it just depends what works best for your organization, both culturally and financially.

Budgeting Cybersecurity Risk

Budgeting for cybersecurity risk is a complex task. Translating risk into dollar amounts, be it for hiring, technology, programs, and/or training, is an in-depth process. And translating risk is not the only decoding activity cybersecurity budgets require—explaining the additional line item to the powers that be is a necessary evil, too.

The fundamental question is: How do you get someone else to buy you something you want? An example might be a teenager who wants her parents to buy her a car.

Before we get to that specific example, let's look at what goes into the decision-making process when you buy a car for yourself. The two principal components are cost and use. Cost is often the principal limiting factor. Most people cannot afford the cars at the high end of the cost spectrum. When you get to $70,000, many people will have dropped out, and $100,000 sports cars and million-dollar supercars are out of reach for most people. But use plays a factor as well. Do you need transportation for one, or do you need room for multiple people? Do you need to carry cargo, or a family, or is it just you? An individual who commutes to work will often buy a different vehicle than will a family that hauls kids to soccer practice and goes on weekend trips to the beach.

But setting aside cost and use, let's look at a seventeen-year-old who wants her parents to buy her a car. Even if we presume the parents can easily afford a $25,000 mid-size sedan (so cost and use is irrelevant), what could possibly motivate them to buy her a car—something she probably does not need?

If she focuses on why she wants the car or how she will use a car, she'll fail. Even if she lists out what she'll do and not do, she'll fail because this approach is all about her. To succeed, she needs to identify how having a car makes her parents better off—she needs to focus on them. She might begin by listing how much time her parents spend carting her around to the various places she needs to go (school, sports practice, Scouts, etc.).

If she's astute, she'll include waiting time, both for her and her parents. To go further, she might list the chores that a seventeen-year-old can take over from her parents (groceries, dry cleaning, hauling younger siblings, taking grandma shopping). Maybe these are things she doesn't want to do, but that's part of the point. If she had money to buy the car on her own, she wouldn't need to convince her parents to pay for it. And trade-offs often mean swapping services for money.

If she makes a compelling case for things that will save her parents time and aggravation, then the other things, the real reasons she wants the car, will put her over the top. And why does she actually want the car? Same reason everybody wants a car—freedom. The freedom to go where she chooses when she chooses—the control which comes from the ability to decide and execute a decision. And her parents certainly want these things for her—just like your Chief Financial Officer (CFO) wants everyone to be safe. But you don't get there, any more than the seventeen-year-old does, if you don't address the CFO's interests first.

And by focusing on her parents' interests, what is she actually doing? She's participating in the broader activities of the family. She's moving herself from the role of a kid (a cost center) to participating in the functions needed to run the family (a profit center). She's making herself a profit center in the business of running the family.

How then, does this work in the security world?

Many cybersecurity teams, whether they have an in-house Security Operations Center (SOC), a complex structure of CISOs, IT leads, engineers and architects, or a two-person unit, struggle to validate their budget. Budget-related seminars, webinars, blogs, and articles direct attention to the importance of identifying stakeholders and asking them what they want the cybersecurity team to do. This advice points us in the right direction, but is fundamentally the wrong approach. We think the advice is well-intentioned, and certainly, it is important to listen to opinions across the enterprise. The problem with the proposed approach is it requires the stakeholder to do all the work—to develop and articulate what they might need in terms of cybersecurity work, which they (typically) know very little about. It is also fraught with risk for the stakeholder to provide a specific answer. As soon as you add the service, and the budget request to support the service goes out, the stakeholder's budget will be sought as the source of those funds. Consequently, asking stakeholders what they need puts them on the spot for an answer and puts their budget at risk if they do tell you.

A much better approach is for certain members of the cybersecurity team to do the heavy lifting. Every service produced by the cybersecurity organization should save the company money. As explained earlier in this chapter, and as Andrea points out here, cybersecurity should not just save the company money—it should be a true value-add:

> **Andrea:** Over the last few years, the CIO role has changed. The discussion has changed. It has moved from a gadget discussion to the value-added services the IT organization can provide, not only for our internal teams but for our external clients. We are now part of the discussion on growing revenue, expanding capabilities, and providing solutions where we can differentiate ourselves against our competitors. We are valued business partners, no longer the siloed IT Department.[24]

This is a sentiment you have and will continue to see echoed by leaders in the cybersecurity space. Stewart Gibson,[25] the Senior Vice President and CIO of USI Insurance Services, confirms Andrea Markstrom's thoughts:

> **Stewart:** IT used to be perceived as a cost center and back-office operation. Today, it does not resemble that at all. Technology is very much customer-facing and perceived as a key to revenue generation. I think it is a terrific shift, and really provides a lot of value and excitement for our IT employees, me included.[26]

---

[24] A. Markstrom, in discussion with the authors. June 24, 2020.

[25] S. Gibson has been with USI since 2006 and has over twenty-five years of experience managing technology organizations from start-ups to Fortune 500 businesses.

[26] S. Gibson, in discussion with the authors. July 27, 2020.

Every company must remember cybersecurity is part of the business. Even if the business lines don't think it is—and at first, they won't—cybersecurity teams must always recognize and ensure their staff functions as part of the business. If you're not part of the business, you're not part of the company. How does that work? Andrea Markstrom illustrates clearly:

> **Andrea:** Whether you are the managing chair, or practice group leader, associate, or legal administrative assistant, there are unique needs from all different roles within the firm. It is important to meet and hear everything, to understand and listen to all feedback. I call it my "listening campaign." It's critical to find out how we as an IT organization do, what we do well, what we need to improve upon. What didn't work well, what they need; not necessarily how we can help them, because I find when I ask them that question they don't know how to respond, but that's where, between myself and my IT leaders, we can make that translation as long as we understand their pain points, what they are struggling with, what is their wish list. I always ask that too—"What's your wish list?"—so I can make that translation. But I think it is so important to know your customer, know your business, so that instills confidence from them in you as their CIO. If you're listening to them, and asking them for their feedback and insights and bringing them along as a partner, that goes a long way. Instead of calling you for a gadget discussion, like what type of mobile phone should I get, the conversation changes to now, "I'm working with a client and we need a solution to a business problem. Can you help us?"[27]

"Andrea's listening campaign" is not a pro forma exercise designed to signal her interest in what the other roles in the firm are doing so she can get "buy in" on her programs later. She is actually taking the time to learn how the rest of the company functions. She wants to understand their pain points so she can make an attempt to solve or help solve them. She's

---

[27] A. Markstrom, in discussion with the authors. June 24, 2020.

actually learning the business. And her questioning process is a key part of how she interacts. She never asks: "How can I help," but rather always asks "What's on your wish list?" And then she translates their wish list into something she can do to solve one of their problems. She'll get the budget because she's doing the problem-solving work.

The issue which prevents most security budgets from being approved is Return On Investment (ROI). To have a chance at getting funded, a safety program must show value received for the money spent. But if the money spent prevents injury, there's no way to show the ROI. Right?

Wrong.

The first thing to get past is the notion that it's impossible to determine the present cost of a future event. The process is actually well established and well known—it's what actuaries do for insurance companies. Your car insurance premium is generated based on actuarial processes which determine the present cost of variable futures which include the possibility, but not certainty of a collision.

The second thing to get past is the notion that the ROI for a security spend which prevents a future event from happening can never be proved. Showing the ROI for a security program which prevents a future event is a two-step process: first, compare the current cost of a given risk vector against the current cost of the same risk vector when reduced by the security program you need funded; second, compare the cost of the security program against the cost reduction found in step one.

This may sound complex, but in practice, it becomes straightforward. Here's an example:

A public road runs between your company's parking lot and office building. There's a crosswalk, but you want to hire a crossing guard for the morning and afternoon rush. A local company will provide the service for $35,000 per year. How do you show ROI?

Your data collection shows that your fifty employees do 24,000 crossings per year. Without a crossing guard on average, one employee per quarter is hit by a car with a cost of $15,000 in medical bills and lost work time per incident. The local service provider has data which shows that with a crossing guard, the incidence drops to one employee per year.

Consequently, the spend of $35,000 reduces the estimated cost of employee injury from $60,000 per year to $15,000 per year, a savings of $45,000 and an ROI of twenty-eight percent. If there are no incidents in a given year, the savings is $60,000 and an ROI of seventy-one percent.

Yes, this is imprecise. Yes, it's a rough estimate. But it will get you much further than requesting funding for a crossing guard because "we need to keep our people safe."

The most difficult part of this example is translating personal injury into funding. And that's the most significant challenge with security budgets: changing the mindset. Most people, even in security, don't look at security from a budget standpoint. They look at security from a safety standpoint, and in doing so, they stop short of the reason why we have security and safety regulations and programs. The reason is simple: no matter what your company does, the company will damage property and injure people in the ordinary course of the company's business. It's a fact, no matter how you mitigate, property will be damaged, and people will be injured. The choice is how much to budget on prevention and how much to budget on remediation. And fortunately for security experts, prevention is almost always less expensive than remediation.

The problem is that most people, including security experts, maintain the belief that security is purely a cost center and always will be. The truth is, the inevitable property damage and injury is the cost center, and by focusing on mitigation and thereby reducing the cost of damage and injury remediation the mindset can change, and security can be seen as a profit center which supports the business. Appreciation of the value of security is necessary, as Amanda explains:

Amanda: The approach to budget has evolved over the years. Our CEO has a strong understanding of technology, the importance of information security, and potential for losses without effective information security. Overall, our C-Suite sees the value, and it's not always that simple for other organizations. Viewing cyber-security as a "cost center" is a little short-sighted. If you have a breach, what are your organization's potential losses, what is the reputational risk; what other financial losses will you suffer by not prioritizing a budget that supports effective cybersecurity?[28]

Your success in getting the funding you need depends on finding ways to articulate this thinking in language which makes sense for your company. It begins with recognizing that no matter what security does, it's an enabler—it's always about the company—and its purpose is to support the business lines. And it begins with the reasons you have security components in the first place. The reason you do everything from updating your software to having people checking IDs at the door is to prevent something bad from happening. And the reason you don't want bad things to happen is so you don't have to pay to fix the damage. And it's the fix which is the genesis of the mindset change: Although security programs prevent people from being hurt and property from being damaged, the company is not doing these things to prevent damage or injury from a sense of altruism. The company has security and safety programs, so the company doesn't have to pay to fix the damage and injury. Security programs protect the company from getting sued, being held liable, and being required to pay damages. To become a profit center and serve the company as it should, security programs must look for and prevent liability.

The best illustration of what happens when security fails to look for liability comes from an unlikely and tragic story: the MGM Grand shooting. On October 1, 2017, a man loaded an arsenal of weapons and ammunition into two rooms at the MGM Grand Resort & Casino in Las Vegas. During the final act of a music festival, he broke open the windows and opened fire from the thirty-second floor into a crowd of concert goers below. He killed fifty-eight people and caused the injury of 869 others in just ten minutes of shooting.[29] How did this happen to a casino? They have a deep understanding of security and they're not a soft target. So how did they miss? They missed because they focused on the wrong thing. In the security world, experts look for "flags"—known precursor

---

[28] A. Tilley, in discussion with the authors. July 02, 2020.

[29] B. Allyn. October 03, 2019. "MGM Resorts to Pay up to $800 Million in Las Vegas Shooting Settlement," *NPR.* www.npr.org/2019/10/03/766800480/mgm-resorts-to-pay-up-to-800-million-to-victims-of-las-vegas-shooting

behaviors that correlate to known violent behaviors. And that's the gap—known flags correlate to known behaviors. What about unknown behaviors? How do you find the thing that's never happened before, the thing nobody has even imagined?

Look for liability. Imagine how different the outcome might have been if, instead of looking for security flags, the strategy was realigned to look at the building as a source of liability. This triggers a new and deeper question: What can happen here that will get us sued? (And if you think this is an unimportant question, remember that the judgment against MGM Grand for its failure was $800 million. Most companies would not survive a judgment that size.)

Viewed from a liability perspective, the risk analysis immediately changes. Everything and every person who goes up into the building is understood more deeply. And it becomes much easier to focus on why one man is renting two rooms on the thirty-second floor and moving up way too many large cargo cases over the course of several days. What's happening here that can get us sued?

The point is this: every business model does things which harm people and damage property. If you look for liability, you'll find everything, including safety issues, and you also protect the company.

How does this matter to your security budget? Michael Woodson explains the process from his former government role:

> **Michael:** Let's take a look at it from the perspective—I'm in government. We have a budget. We have to look at [security] as a need. Now sometimes the business will fund it, or if it's across the enterprise, then we have to budget for them. So how do I talk to the business about it? You have to talk return on investment. So if the control is more expensive to mitigate and bring it forward, it may not be worth it. You have to point out the pros and cons of this to the business, so that they understand what we're talking about from a cost perspective. Even dealing with the CIO and the budget people—if it's too expensive, then it's just not worth it. You're just going to have to ignore it and accept the risk. It's the business case that you're going to attack—the business analysis to show what's the impact.[30]

---

[30] M. Woodson, in discussion with the authors. July 20, 2020.

This brings us back to ROI. It's risk managers and security officers being unable to articulate the ROI for the security spend. How do you bridge this gap?

It begins by translating risk into liability. Rather than speaking in risk management terms (we have a twenty percent chance of getting hit while crossing the street, and getting hit is bad), translate risk into liability (we have a twenty percent chance of incurring $30,000 in medical bills while crossing the street). From this point, translating liability into cost is easy (insurance companies, remember?); it's the actuarial process of pricing the current value of a future event.

So, how does a security director make an effective budget request? Translate the company risk profile into liability categories. Restate every risk in the profile in terms of how likely the company will be sued and what the damages are likely to be. Once a comprehensive set of liability profiles is articulated, pricing the present value of the future events is a matter of math. Once the current cost is established, the mitigation plan can now be adjusted, so the spend for behaviors which reduce risk can be compared to the cost of the risk without mitigation.

Building a budget cycle for risk vectors which are more complex than a crossing guard requires a bit more depth, but there's a strategy. Use the Security Budget Analytic (SBA) loop. It doesn't have the detail or precision of an actuary, but it will provide an estimate accurate enough to support your budget request for any risk vector.

The complete analytic process is illustrated below:

Cost   Behavior

Liability   Risk

Build your plan in three phases.

Phase 1: Current insurance coverage. Look at the risk vectors you already have insured. What can you do to reduce the chance of an incident on those vectors? What can you do to reduce the cost of an incident? The technology, training, and hiring practices which change behavior to reduce risk, liability, and cost become the components of your security program.

Phase 2: Current risk assessment. Use the SBA Loop to analyze each component of your current risk assessment. With the vectors that actually lead to damages, what can you do to reduce both the chance and cost of an incident? This further informs your security program. If you find vectors that don't lead to damages, remove that component from your security program. Don't mitigate because there's no ROI.

Phase 3: Take a broad look at liability. In a general sense, liability is the chance of being sued. Consider all of the ways the company could get sued. The key to this process is understanding that all business models cause harm. No matter what a company does, it injures people and damages property. Those are your liability vectors. Build any new vectors identified in this phase into your risk assessment. Review how the company has been sued in the past and then consider how the company might possibly be sued in the future. What in our business model can (not will, can) damage property and injure people? What have we missed by just looking for risk and by just buying insurance coverage that's offered?

The key is to identify all possible risk vectors, estimate the liability which flows from the risk, and then translate liability into cost. Your ROI is found by comparing the cost of changing behavior (technology, training, and hiring practices) with the reduction in the present cost of your liability as a result of the behavior change.

By starting with the present cost of a variable future event and then moving through the SBA analytic loop, showing the impact of a particular safety program to change behavior and reduce the present cost of the same variable future outcome becomes straightforward.

This process resonates much more deeply once you run your own numbers through the cycle. And remember, security should be serious value-add! As T.J. Harrington,[31] who was Associate Deputy Director of the FBI and then Managing Director and CISO for Citi before his current role as a Senior Advisor with McKinsey & Company, explains through an anecdote of his creation and implementation of world-class Cyber Fusion Centers:

> **T.J.:** One of the things I asked early on at Citi is, "Why aren't we having the opportunity to spend time with clients? Why aren't the bankers and the investment managers wanting to introduce the information security people into their discussions?" Well, at first even my tech guys all said, "No, that's not our responsibility," and I would say, "Yeah, but it's an asset that we have here [the Cyber Fusion Center]. We're creating something that's so unique, and it's on the top of every executives' mind in these other businesses." Eventually I spent time with some of the investment guys, and they agreed to introduce me into those discussions. It became a business development effort. I mean it exploded. In fact, my boss was freaking out because we were seeing so many clients coming through, but what it was actually doing was fulfilling the mission that I first presented to the CEO, which was, "We want to increase our wallet share with clients. We want to form greater and stronger business relationships with them." So, by sharing with them our strategy, showing them the things we were doing and spending a few hours with them in the fusion center, we ended up being a business developer.[32]

T.J.'s now famous transformative approach to cybersecurity at Citi allowed the financial institution to use its cutting edge capabilities as a selling point to international clients. While not every company has this opportunity, T.J.'s work underscores the importance of understanding how to best discuss cybersecurity budgets and ROI.

---

[31] T.J. Harrington was appointed Associate Deputy Director of the FBI by Robert Mueller, after serving as the Executive Assistant Director of the Criminal, Cyber, Response, and Services Branch. After his service with the FBI, T.J. joined Citi as the Managing Director and CISO. Currently, T.J. is a Senior Advisor at McKinsey and Company.

[32] T.J. Harrington, in discussion with the authors. July 31, 2020.

CHAPTER 2

Can–Trust–Will

Can–Trust–Will is our model for hiring. While the rest of this book focuses on how to apply it to cybersecurity hiring, this chapter focuses on the model itself—with a bird's-eye view of each piece. Call it a funnel, call it a multilayered process—but in the end, these are each filters that are geared to get you to the right candidate.

An Overview of Can–Trust–Will

Each phase of *Can–Trust–Will* requires attention and accuracy in order to make the system work effectively and efficiently. Most of the job search and most of the model will not be about looking for and finding an individual. There's a reason the job search has three phases; it's not an outright hunt for an individual. When using this model, you must understand that it begins by assembling and filtering candidate pools, not just by searching for someone. The right candidate pools, correctly assembled and filtered, will produce the right candidates for final differentiation in a behavioral interview. Correctly done, the process of assembling and then filtering pools of candidates down to the individuals who should be interviewed will identify the particular individual you need to hire.

This may sound counterintuitive, but you're actually not looking for an individual candidate until very late in the process. For most of your talent search, the focus should be on building candidate pools and then extracting from those candidate pools more refined, smaller candidate pools. Once you have a sufficient understanding of who you're looking at, then you can start looking at individuals, but not before.

And the order of the pools is crucial. *Can–Trust–Will* begins with the easiest differentiators and ends with the most difficult. Why? Because easy is also inexpensive, while difficult requires time, expertise, and money. So this process begins by filtering the largest candidate pools for capabilities which are easy to assess and delays the more expensive and time inten-sive data extraction for the smaller, more refined candidate pools. The last thing your budget needs is a hiring process which runs expensive assessment processes on large numbers of applicants who have no realistic possibility of getting a job offer. Start with *Can*.

Phase One—Can: This is the process of filtering the initial candidate pool for technical skill. Do they have the technical competence required for the job opening? This is simple, not because the job skillset is simple, but because the assessment is binary. Can the candidates actually do the technical stuff, or can't they. And since it's binary, the method doesn't matter too much as long as it tests the skills you need. It might be a writ-ten test, or a practical assessment—hand them a device and watch how they fix it—or it might be an interview. But the sole focus is to determine technical skill.

And the key is to resist the temptation to do more "while the candi-date is here." The notion that you will save money and be more efficient by bringing everybody in one time and running them through everything from skills tests to behavioral interviews is an expensive mistake. And it also leads to making The Big Mistake which we address in detail in Chapter 4.

Remember, you're building pools. And you're building pools for the purpose of quickly, accurately, and inexpensively filtering for the indi-vidual who will actually succeed in this specific role at your company. The first pool necessarily includes all the people in the world you could find who are interested in this job, and consequently, your first step is to separate out the people who can actually, technically, do the job. And you're going to do that binary assessment as quickly and inexpen-sively as you possibly can. And if that means candidates come in just to do a short interview or a quick test that is specifically focused on the last time they debugged a Cisco stack, or to tell a story about when they did this, that, or the other technical thing—that's fine. Remem-ber, it's a high-volume process. You'll be assessing many candidates, so the key is to ensure it's very quick, very simple, and very focused on technical competency.

And once you have your smaller pool of candidates who *Can* do the work, you move on to identifying those you can *Trust*. Most of the industry already hires based on *Can*, and consequently, many companies will already have some process in place to make the assessment. Do that, but recognize you're not done at that point. Companies which only hire on *Can* quickly face high turnover because they don't understand anything about their candidates other than their technical capability. And technical capability, by itself, does not correlate to job success. It is crucial to understand who the candidate is—can he or she be trusted, and what are his or her behaviors that will lead to success in the role. In order to gain this deeper understanding, a deeper dive into both background and behavior must be completed. Background is *Trust*; behavior is *Will*.

Phase Two—Trust: Once you have identified the subset pool of candidates who can actually do the work, the process of understanding "who are these candidates" can begin. Again, the key is to do the simple, inexpensive differentiation first so that the deeper, more expensive, and time-consuming examination can be done on fewer people. Understanding each candidate begins with the simplest forms of due diligence. And although *Trust* encompasses everything from basic public records checks all the way over to a determination of ethical code and moral compass, the process of layered review which structures the overall *Can–Trust–Will* process is also used to structure the variety of due diligence processes which are included in the *Trust* phase.

Determining how deep to go and how much time and money to devote to a given candidate in the *Trust* phase is driven by the specifics of the job description, and in particular the access which comes from each job and how much harm an employee can do to the company from that position. For example, someone who checks identification and enters guest information into the security system has much less access and can do much less harm to the company than a systems administrator who has root access to that same security system. Consequently, a criminal records check is likely to be sufficient for the employee who enters data while a much deeper background investigation is warranted for the systems administrator.

The key is, it's layered. Simple and inexpensive records checks are done for less risky job roles, and more complex, time consuming, and expensive background reviews are done for higher risk job roles. The time and resources dedicated to each individual vary but are driven by the risk inherent to the job role. Ethics and moral compass are relevant here because they are relevant to corporate culture and transition us to the final filter. Moral compass and ethics are some of the drivers of behavior, because what you value influences the things you do. In that way, we transition from the deep end of *Trust* to the shallow end of *Will*. And *Will* matters, because it predicts behavior, and behavior leads either to success or failure.

Phase Three—Will: This phase is a deep dive past the generic reliability characteristics which are extracted in the *Trust* phase. In the *Will* phase, there are many fewer candidates and the focus is now on behavior. What *Will* the candidate do in the future? Behaviors are the characteristics of a person which drive that person's actions. And that's really the core purpose of this hiring system. To identify an individual who has (or can learn) the technical skill and will also behave in a manner which enhances the functioning of the company regardless of whether it's an ordinary day or one where everything comes crashing down and the stress level is through the roof.

The processes used in the *Will* phase are based on two premises: first, there is an observable difference between what a person is capable of doing (what they *Can* do), and what they actually do when they show up for work (what they *Will* do). Furthermore, what a person *Will* do is not linear. The fact that a person will do exactly what's needed under normal circumstances does not mean that they will continue to do what is needed when stressors arise. *Will* is complex because it is affected by circumstances, and circumstances change, sometimes very quickly. Whether there's a crisis situation at work or they've got a parent in the hospital—what a person actually does under stress varies without relation to what they do under normal circumstances.

Second, the best predictor of future behavior is past behavior. And the key to understanding past behavior is the behavioral interview. The process is to ask the few candidates who have passed all of the filters and made it through to the interview to share stories from their past which will demonstrate how they previously behaved in situations which are similar to what you anticipate they will encounter when working for you. In evaluating the stories the candidate shares, you will be able to assess whether the candidate possesses the behaviors which correlate to success in the specific job role at your company. The behavioral interview, the final phase, is time consuming, is expensive, and requires a good level of skill by the interviewer. Consequently, it should not be done for a large volume of candidates—only for the candidates who have a reasonable probability of success, and only at the end of the process immediately before the hiring, decision is made.

In addition, behaviors are extremely job specific, so the behavioral interview must focus on the specific set of behaviors which correlate to success in the job role. To properly prepare for a behavioral interview requires that you know, at a granular level, what behaviors correlate to success and which to failure for each specific job. There is no universal set of behaviors that a cybersecurity or IT person needs. Thus, the *Will* phase requires a thoughtful approach to drafting a job description, including both *Can* and *Will* factors—capabilities and behaviors—for each role. Even though it requires resources and skill, the behavioral interview allows the interviewer to understand and analyze what behaviors the candidate possesses—the good and the (potentially) negative—and differentiates between what the candidate *Can* do, in contrast to what they *Will* do and thereby drives the best possible hiring decision.

Now that we've described the *Can–Trust–Will* structure, and before we take a deeper dive into each component, we'd like to spend a moment on how to assess. Many of the experts who have contributed to this book are concerned with learning, particularly the value of candidates who have the ability to learn quickly, and those who are tinkerers, who have the curiosity to figure out complex problems, and who are unafraid to break things so they can figure out how to fix them. The question generally posed is related to high-potential candidates. What is the best outcome for candidates who fail the technical skills evaluation, or even some components of the behavioral interview? Is it best to summarily reject these candidates, or is there a better way?

Our better way is to take binary outcomes (Can or Can't) and divide the rejection outcome into those who can probably be trained and those who probably can't. Welcome to Failure–Coachable, Failure–Noncoachable, and Success.

An Overview of Assessment: Failure–Coachable, Failure–Noncoachable, and Success

So far in our overview of *Can–Trust–Will*, we have described the things which must be assessed and the order in which they should be examined. Now we take a minute to discuss how to assess. Running through the system doing binary evaluations will result in some candidates being accepted but many others being summarily notified that they do not meet the requirements and will not be considered further. The concern is whether such a strict system will result in good candidates being rejected when just a bit of improvement or training would produce an excellent employee. How do we ensure we don't miss good candidates who just need an assist?

Binary assessment—pass/fail—is efficient, and not digging deeper is a defensible decision, particularly in the *Can* phase where there may be a large volume of people who meet the standard and are capable of doing the technical work. In that case, digging deeper to assist marginal candidates is probably not cost-effective or worthwhile. But if there are not a sufficient volume of candidates with the technical skill or if you are in the *Will* phase and are disqualifying every candidate, it is worth digging deeper to determine if a candidate can be trained or coached to success.

This deeper assessment requires an evaluation of potential. If a candidate cannot or will not do what is necessary right now, is it possible they will be able to in the future? Is a currently unqualified candidate trainable? Can the deficit be remedied by learning? Is the candidate coachable? To fully assess potential, there are two aspects to consider. First, can the particular candidate learn? Not everyone can learn and not everyone is willing to learn. Furthermore, the reality is that not everybody can learn quickly, or quickly enough. Second, and more importantly, is the deficit something which can be taught? Many deficits can be corrected through training, but there are some things which people are bad at which probably can't be taught. Potential depends on whether the candidate is a learner and on whether the specific deficit can be remedied by training. And that is the beginning of the dichotomy between Failure–Coachable and Failure–Noncoachable. It's a question of identifying weaknesses but also making a judgment regarding potential to correct the weakness.

Can this person learn this thing or can they not? The simplest example we usually turn to is: I can probably teach you how to drive a forklift, but I probably can't teach you how to be on time. And that's the difference between Failure–Coachable and Failure–Noncoachable—to make sure that you are capturing the people who are going to be great if they have training, and separating those from the people who are not going to improve from training.

A more complex example is something like writing a meeting agenda. Some people can learn how to do it, but some people actually can't. If you have a person who loves the chaos of an unstructured conversation, you can tell them that agendas are important and you can explain to them that a free and easy conversational style is great in a poker game, but it doesn't produce the results you need in a professional business setting, but they probably will never learn how to do an agenda and keep decision making on track during a business meeting. It may be that they simply can't do it, or it may be that they won't do it because they'd rather have the free conversation they like instead of the structured conversation the business needs. But since it's unlikely to happen, regardless of the cause, their inability to write a meeting agenda can't be solved by training, and the potential for their success in such a role is very low. They are Failure–Noncoachable. On the other hand, if you have a person who has never structured a meeting agenda before, and it takes them six hours to do what should only take twenty minutes—but they actually do it—that person has learning potential. What we have seen is if the person understood the process, if they learned, the first time it took six hours, but the second time only took three hours, and by the fourth iteration, they were doing it faster than the supervisor. That's a person with high potential for success in such a role. They are Failure–Coachable.

Spotlight: Digging Deeper Into Coachable Versus Noncoachable

The distinction between coachable and noncoachable can be delicate and layered and requires thorough analysis. We were recently called to assist a client with a new hire who had been identified as a high-potential leadership candidate and immediately placed into the client's leader development pipeline. Spots in the program were limited and highly coveted, and this employee—who had been assessed as a top performer—was now failing out. The company wanted to know why. We conducted a 360-interview and evaluation process which revealed the employee was highly intelligent, capable of learning the system materials, and interested in the benefits of promotion. However, when presented with the additional workload required by the leader development pipeline program, he would consistently delay doing the assignments, request an extension, and then when pressed, would present reasons for failing to complete the additional work. We quickly realized his reasons were carefully curated to fit within HR policies which made it impossible for the company to take corrective action. So he stayed in the program taking up valuable resources while making no progress toward completion. Our evaluation concluded that the candidate possessed the intelligence and skills to succeed in the program but was simply unwilling to do the work. While we were impressed by his highly skilled passive avoidance techniques, we assessed him as Failure–Noncoachable.

Further illustrative of this concept is a situation where an executive coaching client was struggling in her role as Chief Operating Officer at a medium-sized company. She had been successful in a variety of developmental roles, which had led to a promotion. Her boss wanted to "get her some help" and to remedy "her tendency to micromanage." After a few months of coaching sessions, we found she didn't actually micromanage: she did all the work. As her career had progressed, she succeeded by working harder than her contemporaries, coming in earlier and leaving later, and taking pride in being a "workaholic." While that strategy had been effective in the earlier developmental roles, it failed her in the Chief Operating Officer because there were not enough hours in the day to do everything herself. Things progressively fell apart as the tasks for which she was responsible exceeded her bandwidth. Unfortunately, she continued to insist that it was her job to do everything. She believed that a fundamental part of her role as an executive was to come up with the best ideas. If her staff came up with an idea, she used it—but considered it to be a personal failure. In her mind, and her self-image, she had the most experience and skill so she should be coming up with everything. If someone of lesser skill and experience solved a problem, it was because she had failed. Consequently, she was incapable of focusing on ensuring operations were completed because she was fully engaged with doing everything. And she could not understand why she was being criticized when she was working so hard. Because of this perspective, she was fundamentally unable to understand why operations were failing. She was also incapable of understanding that her staff was unhappy because they had to wait for her authority to do even the most basic tasks, which meant they waited for extended periods to get basic approvals because she was so busy. We assessed her as Failure–Noncoachable. A person either has the ability to acknowledge skill in another without being threatened, or they don't—she did not. Allowing others to succeed lowered her self-image. A person with this attitude may be able to change, but it usually comes as an epiphany; it's not something that can be taught.

On the opposite end of the spectrum, a client came to us from the culinary industry. She had landed a job in a prestigious restaurant right out of culinary school and was building a successful career in this male-dominated field. However, she was preparing to quit because of how frustrating her work situation had become after a recent promotion. She had been given supervisory responsibility for two entry-level chefs, and they would simply not do their jobs. As a consequence, our client was regularly disciplined for the errors caused by her charges; she found that all she wanted to do was scream at them even though she knew it wouldn't help. Through the course of a ten-week coaching program, we began a process of learning about the details of her situation and suggesting strategies to try. Nearly all of our guidance was focused on helping her to understand the behavioral characteristics of her charges and to develop strategies which caused them to face immediate negative consequences for bad behavior and immediate positive consequences for good behavior (all without her needing to scream). One of the things which impressed us the most about this client was how hard she pressed us for explanations about our advice and for detail regarding how to interact in alternative scenarios. Her most common question was: "Yeah, but how … ?" She wanted to succeed, and as some of the strategies began to work, she deepened her questioning. In short, she had a high level of willingness to try a variety of different things, evaluate results, then refine, and refine, and refine again. When we picked up the phone for our week eight conversation, she announced she had been promoted to middle management. A year later, she was promoted again and this time to sous-chef. Going from screaming frustration to a double promotion simply based on a willingness to try anything new to see if it worked, and to keep refining until it did work, is Failure–Coachable.

This dichotomy can now be applied to one of the most common issues in cybersecurity, which is communication. Specifically, the use of technical terms; the notion of "speaking tech" versus "speaking people." If you have a person who can both "speak tech" and "speak people," but they won't lower themselves to "speak people," the issue is *Will*—and the question to answer in assessing potential is whether the candidate is responsive enough to a coaching conversation to change their opinion and choose to "speak people" when it's needed. If the person responds positively to a discussion of when technical jargon is useful and when it creates problems, they are Failure–Coachable. They may need a series of reminder conversations to reinforce their improvement trajectory, but the problem can be remedied through coaching because they are willing to change and "speak people" when it's necessary. On the other hand, if the response is "Yes, I can 'speak people.' But I shouldn't have to. So I won't." That choice is Failure–Noncoachable. Such a person may change his or her mind over time, particularly if a negative consequence is involved, such as reassignment to a role which does not require interaction with nontechnical personnel. But training isn't going to help, so training is a waste of time and resources. Another example is teamwork: if a person knows how to operate in a team environment, they will rate high in a teamwork personality assessment—but it only matters when things get stressful and/or if in the day-to-day if they want to work in a team environment.

And that raises one of the high-impact issues with Failure–Coachable in the cybersecurity world: the time and expense of training and coaching. In addition to the expense of some types of technical training, the industry is currently struggling with an inability to reliably predict aptitude for cybersecurity training and skill development. This raises a complex set of decisions which are driven by a variety of factors. Employer size and financial capability is an overarching factor which drives different companies to handle candidates with a lack of skill and training in different ways. A large company with a great need for entry-level employees will be more able to place new hires into a training program and be minimally impacted by those who fail out or discover they don't have the aptitude to learn the skills necessary to perform jobs in the cybersecurity realm. Smaller companies don't have the budget or time to have an in-house training program. Consequently, a Failure–Coachable candidate has a better chance of being hired in a low-level job with a very large company and a very poor chance of being hired by a two-person firm who needs an expert who can immediately begin to serve the client they just landed.

The concept of distinguishing between Failure–Coachable and Failure–Noncoachable has broad application to both hiring and job performance in the technical world, in general, and the cybersecurity arena, in particular. In general, skill can be taught, attitude can't (this goes back to the forklift/being-on-time example). Why is this import-ant? Because, particularly in cybersecurity, not every applicant will come to you fully developed in the way that you need them. If your process disqualifies everyone who has a high level of failure indicators, you'll not only miss people you should hire, you'll miss the opportunity to team build through training. But it's critical when differentiating between Failure–Coachable and Failure–Noncoachable to ensure you only con-sider people with attributes which can actually be trained. Hiring an oth-erwise great candidate with the hope that they will somehow become inspired to show up on time (for example) is futile. On the other hand, hiring someone who has passion for the work and is eager to learn but does not have the technical skill to do the job is not really a risk. It's a training issue to be addressed during onboarding. The key is to distin-guish between those who will progress through training and those who will not. Marie Chudolij,[1] a Senior Program Manager for Siemplify, a security operations provider, expressed it simply:

> **Marie:** You can teach people how to do things, but you can't teach people how to behave or change their personality. You can review

---

[1] With more than twelve years of experience working in IT and project manage-ment, Marie Chudolij is currently a Senior Program Manager at Siemplify. She works in the Security, Orchestration, Automation, and Response (SOAR) space, overseeing the implementation of automation for Security Operation Center (SOC) procedures and workflows.

a resumé and it looks like they're going to be a rockstar, but when you have an opportunity to sit down with them, the personality may not necessarily be quite right. I honestly feel that personality is going to be far more important than your previous experience. Because I can teach most people how to follow new processes or work with new programs, but I can't change who they are.[2]

As Marie explains, there is a fundamental difference between what a person can do and how they will behave. In fact, the Failure–Coachable category was created to address what to do with great people who need training. Failure–Noncoachable is the repository for those who have the skill but lack the ability to implement through interaction. Bill Brennan,[3] the Senior Director of Global Information Security at Leidos, reinforces this point:

> **Bill:** I can't change your gray matter. You are who you are. I can probably modify some of your behaviors, but your experiences make you who you are. I can teach you technical skills. I'm confident that if I think you're smart and you're capable and you have the right nature for the role that we're looking for, I can teach you the technical bit.[4]

Bill's observations match our experience. Who you are is driven by what you value, and your values dictate your behavior; essentially, how you choose to act, or more precisely, how you choose to interact. The key is to identify, as early as possible, the need for training. That's why *Can*—capability and skill—come first. And why *Will*—what Bill calls "gray matter"—is the final step. Capability and skill are much more susceptible to correction by training; how a person chooses to act, much less

---

[2] M. Chudolij, in discussion with the authors. July 24, 2020.
[3] Prior to joining Leidos as the Senior Director of Global Information Security, Bill Brennan was part of Lockheed Martin's Global Cyber Practice, where he became Managing Director of the Global Cyber and Intelligence Practice, working with government and private clients.
[4] B. Brennan, in discussion with the authors. August 04, 2020.

so. Amanda affirms this view, explaining why cybersecurity is so unique in this aspect:

> **Amanda:** In my opinion, information security is ultimately risk management. Sure, you need to have the technical understanding and layers of controls and tools to identify, protect, detect, respond, and recover, but at its core, information security manages the risk to the confidentiality, integrity, and availability of an organization's information. That understanding sets you apart in infosec; you can learn the technical aspects. It's those innate traits of wanting to learn, wanting to solve the puzzle, an ability to communicate clearly, keep calm under pressure, and a strong moral compass—that you need to be successful in information security.[5]

Some may be uncomfortable with the term "failure" as being unduly pejorative. In the absence of an equally clear term, we believe "failure" is appropriate. Particularly, when divided into "Failure–Coachable" and "Failure–Noncoachable." But there is another reason which is relevant to security in general and to cybersecurity in particular. This is a high stress world. We expect the people in these jobs to act quickly, clearly, and accurately when everything is crashing down around them. We expect them to be able to put the business first and themselves second. We filter for the ability to give bad news to someone much higher in the chain of command, someone who can damage their career or fire them, simply because accurately describing how bad things are is crucial to solving the problem, but is also simply the right thing to do. In essence, we are looking for resilient and mature professionals. As Nick Davis,[6] the Director of Information Security Governance Risk and Compliance for the University of Wisconsin System, explains:

---

[5] A. Tilley, in discussion with the authors. July 02, 2020.

[6] Nick Davis serves as the Director of Information Security Governance Risk and Compliance for the University of Wisconsin System, and has over twenty-five years of experience working in the field of information security in both the public and private sectors, with extensive expertise in public key cryptography systems.

Nick: When I interview people, I look at their outlook on things. Are they optimistic in nature, are they kind, or do they seem aggressive? Do they seem thoughtful, do they seem anxious? And I look for those general personality attributes because information security is a frustrating field to work in. I'm looking to see if they can maintain a calm demeanor, can they stick to their convictions while they're maintaining their calm demeanor. You don't want people that are just people pleasers. You want people who can remain calm and polite, but people that don't move easily from their convictions.[7]

One of the markers of resilient and mature professionals is to not be derailed by failure, to be able to look past failure, to learn from it, and to be hungry to "fail forward." If you can't get past having failures (because they will happen to everyone in this field), then you probably will not succeed in the high-pressure environment of cybersecurity. Differentiating between Failure–Coachable and Failure–Noncoachable is actually how we distinguish between a candidate who is comfortable with the discomfort of failing forward and identifying a candidate who should look for a rewarding career outside of cybersecurity.

Can They Do It?

The *Can* of our hiring model is specifically, one might say narrowly, focused on technical skill. The specifics of *Can* may be uncovered through the resumé, a preliminary interview, or some type of skill testing protocol, but the key is to remember that since it's the first step, it's the biggest candidate pool and therefore the most expensive. To ensure you find the employees you need at the end of the process, and to avoid unfairness and potentially, litigation, whatever evaluation you do for one candidate in each pool, you must do for all of them. Cybersecurity skill evaluation takes many forms. Government competitions, commercial assessments, homegrown corporate testing, skill interviews, cursory resumé reviews

---

[7] N. Davis, in discussion with the authors. July 27, 2020.

(looking just for skill capability)—it depends on the sector, size, and cybersecurity maturity of the hiring entity.

One of the most difficult challenges is having the self-discipline to use resumés properly in this initial phase. So many processes begin with a stack of resumés and quickly devolve into separating them into two stacks: some form of "interview" and "discard." This is fundamentally a waste of time because it does not extract skill data and also leads to a high volume of interviews (usually, all of the "not sures" also get interviewed). If there is a resumé review in the *Can* phase, it simply must be confined to confirming whether the resumé provides data which reveal whether the candidate has the technical skills necessary for the job role. All the reviewer should look for is degrees and prior job experience, nothing more.

Questionnaires sent in advance may be used in place of a *Can*-based, in-person interview. There are many commercial vendors that offer quizzes tailored to general job descriptions (i.e., malware analyst, IT security, and incident responder). These evaluations can consist of twenty-five questions or scenarios requiring analysis that may take four hours. Generally, advanced question sets may be best suited for mature cybersecurity organizations with a large-scale operation. However, this requires a staff of HR professionals with the resources to conduct research upon which to build question sets which correlate to job performance. Such testing may also be done on-site, if the employer prefers—it's the same evaluation.

A key consideration to keep in mind here is the difference between the thought processes which are essentially technical skills and behavioral characteristics which are not. The confusion can come during the *Can* evaluation of highly technical skills for some cybersecurity jobs. Let's begin with a simple example. A candidate who is highly suited to read network traffic logs all day is highly suited to it because they love the structure and process which comes with reading such logs. Reading these logs is fairly simple and most people with a bit of technical training can do it. But only a detail-oriented person who is most comfortable when following procedure is willing to do it all day long. Consequently, the differentiator for a job reading network traffic logs all day is not the technical skill of being able to read these logs; it's the behavioral characteristic of wanting to do it and finding satisfaction in doing it that correlates to job success. This is an issue to be addressed in the behavioral interview done during the *Will* phase, and not indulged in during the initial *Can* phase.

A more difficult example is the evaluation of the thought process which is part of the technical skill set for data analysts. The challenge is that questions that serve to unearth whether a candidate has the problem-solving/analytic thought process capability required for the job role may mimic behavioral interview questions when they're actually not. The confusion arises when the interviewer, quite correctly, asks the candidate to recount a situation which demonstrates her thought process. The difference is in what the interviewer is seeking. For *Can*, the interviewer wants a story about a thought process; for *Will*, the story needs to be about a behavior. How you think is a skill, it's not a behavior. How you interact is a behavior, not a skill.

And while both can be explored, particularly when operating at a sophisticated level, the difference is found in the form of the question. The *Can* question is: "What did you do when you detected malware spreading through a certain sector, assuming this operating system, this software, this [fill-in-the-blank]?" This question wants to know what your brain did. In contrast, the *Will* question is: "Tell us about a time when you uncovered malware on a senior executive's device; what was your incident reporting strategy, and how did you work with your team to stop the spread?" This question seeks out how your feelings impacted your behavior. Alexi Michaels,[8] a trainer-developer at BlackBag Technologies, a computer forensics software company,

> **Alexi:** My boss did not ask me super technical questions—he said he did not like to judge based on putting someone on the spot. But instead he did ask technical questions on what I would do in a certain situation, or how I would conduct a certain type of analysis.[9]

---

[8] Alexi Michaels continues her work in the field of digital forensics, where she has expertly analyzed digital evidence in internal investigations, litigation, and hacking cases. She has a bachelor's degree in Digital Forensics from Bloomsburg University of Pennsylvania, and is currently a trainer-developer at BlackBag Technologies, which was acquired by Cellebrite.

[9] A. Michaels, in discussion with the authors. July 03, 2020.

The *Can*-based interview may also include on-the-spot assessments in the form of real-time scenarios, as Martin Durst,[10] a Senior IT Support Specialist at Drexel University's Kline School of Law, recalls from his own interview experience:

> **Martin:** When I got to the [interview] room only the hiring manager was there. My future team member popped in, he said, "This is perfect," and took me to the office of the Associate Dean of Students, who was having issues with his computer. So my now senior teammate asked me to troubleshoot the Dean's computer. Even though I don't think it was planned this way, it worked out because it became a practical part of the interview. His computer was slow, and I was able to fix it. The Dean, the hiring manager, and my teammate were all very happy, and the rest of the interview went very smoothly.[11]

Whether the Associate Dean's computer slowdown was premeditated or not, the scenario allowed the hiring manager an undoubtedly keen glimpse into Martin's skill set, problem-solving ability, and mindset in handling a problem, thereby going above and beyond the *Can* phase in a few respects. A whiteboard session may serve the same purpose: to help the hiring manager see the candidate's ability, but also her thought process and reactions to stress. As Amanda explains:

> **Amanda:** We conduct whiteboarding sessions as the final interview round for candidates. Nothing overly complicated, but we found that asking a candidate to whiteboard a few simple scenarios helps distinguish the candidates who just know the buzzwords. It also provides insight into how an individual conducts themselves under pressure and how the candidate problem solves. Something I find valuable during an interview is a candidate's willingness to say "I don't know." Humility and self-awareness are important personality traits. Not to just say "I don't know" and wait for

---

[10] Martin Durst is a Senior IT Support Specialist at Drexel University's Kline School of Law. He has a Bachelor of Science in Computer Science and is ITIL: Foundation certified.

[11] M. Durst, in discussion with the authors. June 29, 2020.

someone to give you the answer, but to look for the answer, to talk through their thought process, and knowing when it's time to ask for help. The whiteboarding session has become essential to our hiring process. It's not our intention to get a "gotcha," in fact, I think standing up in front of three people with a marker and a board is pressure enough. The exercise showcases the candidate's skill level in what would be required in their day-to-day, while also getting a better understanding of their personality, rather than the typical formality of an interview.[12]

The *Can* phase of our hiring model necessarily focuses on technical skill. And both Alexi and Martin recount different ways in which data can be extracted to reveal a candidate's level of skill. Amanda's example actually shows something equally important, which is that just because a candidate has already demonstrated *Can*, technical skill-based questions can still be part of the later *Will* review processes. *Will* does not have to be assessed in a vacuum. The whiteboard is the final stage of Amanda's selection process, and while it tests for differential data relevant to behavioral characteristics, it does so in a unified process which places the candidate in a situation where they must show how their technical skill and moral compass interact with their behavioral characteristics under stress and thereby reveal the whole person. By placing the whiteboard session at the end, Amanda conducts a deep, time consuming, and expensive review, but only for the very few candidates who are most likely to succeed. It is wonderful confirmation of the efficiency and cost-effectiveness of the *Can–Trust–Will* process.

Should the Organization Trust Them?

Many people get to some point in the due diligence and insider threat discussion when they say, sometimes in frustration, "But I have to trust my people. Without trust, we can't function." And as far as that statement goes, it's correct; but a deeper understanding of trust in business is warranted. How do we trust in business? How do we build trust in business? And how do we know when we can trust in business? The answer is as simple as it is counterintuitive.

---

[12] A. Tilley, in discussion with the authors. July 02, 2020.

If we look at *Trust* from a due diligence standpoint, we want to do a general review of trustworthiness that is based on past behavior. Does this person lie, cheat, or steal? We answer that question by looking in the past to see whether they've lied, cheated, or stolen before. If we are doing something deeper: will this person be a negative disruptor or will they not—that now becomes a hybrid. Can I trust this person with my innermost thoughts as we are problem solving, or as soon as I say something that they disagree with, are they going to pounce on me? That becomes a trust interaction and very quickly goes to how you have a trust relationship with another person. Here, we distinguish between interpersonal trust and trust in business. The interesting thing about trust in the business and leadership sense is whether a person has a trusting relationship depends on them, not on the person they are trusting. You see this in executive coaching and leadership seminars when they talk about micromanaging.

Trust does not arise because a person is trustworthy, and it does not come when a person demonstrates trustworthiness by establishing a track record of good behavior. Trust can be immediate and has nothing to do with the person being trusted. For business, trust in another person exists when you believe they cannot harm you or your business. When you believe there is nothing a person can break or screw up that you can't fix, you are able to give that person leeway to try, fail forward, and learn. In business, that's trust. Part of true team-building actually starts with the idea that as I interact with my teammates, I know I can say anything because I'm in an environment that doesn't punish me for saying it. And it's also an environment where I can try things because there's no way I can create irreparable harm. Amanda explains how trust allows her team to effectively get the job done:

> **Amanda:** Our team is composed of members with diverse experiences and perspectives. While most of our team has worked in IT, some members worked in customer service, project management, risk management, and some in different industries. Each member's unique perspectives are amplified by our trust for one another to do our best, do what's right, and meet our collective goals. Transparent communication is everything to our team. We've often referred to our team as the "circle of trust"—a reference to Robert

DeNiro in *Meet the Fockers*—we need to trust each other in order to be effective as a team.[13]

This idea is further explored in Chapter 5, on "Trust and Teamwork." If, on the other hand, you think a person can create problems that will be difficult for you to solve or which will create irreparable harm, then you won't trust that person to act without oversight and their track record of good behavior will have no impact on your micromanaging of their work. Business trust rises and falls on your perception of your own ability to handle problems created by others. If you have difficulty with trust at work, the issues to be addressed lie within.

Spotlight: Due Diligence Vetting

Due diligence is not static, it's a process. And like most processes, to be effective, it requires a strategy. So, where do you start? Due diligence has three essential components. They are trade-offs, and there is no way of getting around them. So use them to decide what's important to you and your company, and then make value judgments needed to build your strategy. The three components are speed, accuracy, and cost.

Quick due diligence processes can be either cheap (a down and dirty glimpse) or expensive (lightning fast return), but they are generally less accurate because they are a single snapshot in time. Remember, a records check or data pull is only as good as the database being pulled from, and a single data pull begins getting stale as soon as it's done. Something that happens immediately after your data pull will not be in your results. Slow due diligence processes can also be either cheap (slow results) or expensive (an extensive deep dive), but they will often be more comprehensive because they tend to pull data from several sources over the time frame of the due diligence process. In addition to data pulls, a longer process can include reference interviews, work history confirmation, and other deep dive investigative components.

Expensive due diligence is not necessarily high quality. Sometimes expensive just means labor intensive. And sometimes, it just means

---

[13] A. Tilley, in discussion with the authors. July 02, 2020.

expensive. Accurate due diligence does not necessarily mean expensive. A cheap data pull from an aggregated database which is highly likely to have what you are looking for is both cost-effective and accurate. And cheap due diligence is not necessarily low quality. The low-cost due diligence services usually rely on a data pull from one of the three major data aggregators.

Once you begin to see the level of complexity caused by the trade-offs of speed, accuracy, and cost, you'll understand that expert assistance is a necessity to ensure you don't hire someone who ends up damaging all you have built. Consulting with a reputable firm is a good way to ensure your due diligence process is properly assembled.

Spotlight: Data Aggregators

Knowing who the big data aggregators are and understanding what's in their databases can assist in your strategic decision making.

As of this publication, the three main data aggregators are TransUnion, Thomson Reuters, and Lexis/Nexus. Many of the companies who offer due diligence and background check services use one or several of these data aggregators. Each database has positives and negatives because each aggregator gathers different types of data and refreshes its database at different rates. Most important is to understand that aggregated data are second-hand, so you need to know how accurate it is. For example, if an aggregator advertises that it collects ninety percent of all available data, you risk having the data you need being in the ten percent gap. Next in importance is the refresh rate. Is the aggregated database updated daily? That's great, but also very expensive. Is it updated monthly? Quarterly? That gap means that even if the aggregator collects one hundred percent of available data, it still misses the most recent data and will continue to miss it until the next refresh. Some may think this is a binary choice between buying the most expensive service and doing nothing—but it's not. The key with due diligence records checks is to ensure you know what you're getting for the spend.

If you ensure you know where the gaps in the data are, you can make a choice about whether and how to fill those gaps with other due diligence services. And it's knowing what the gaps are that allows you to utilize due diligence services more effectively in executing your strategy. The key is to understand the data and how it's being searched so you know how to assess the result. And that means asking questions of the search firms you consider hiring. And finally, understand when you hire a search firm that uses aggregated data, it adds a step—a third party is searching a second-hand database. Quick? Yes. Cheap? Certainly. But also potentially inaccurate. When looking at services which use aggregated data, remember the trade-offs: speed, accuracy, and cost.

What's the next step beyond firms which use aggregated data? Many due diligence and investigative firms offer services which conduct public records checks on individuals. Generally, the service needs you to select a time frame and to provide the places where the candidate has lived and worked during that time frame. A basic example would be a five-year check. The company would conduct public records searches by contacting the county and city clerk offices of every jurisdiction where the candidate has lived and worked in the past five years. It's easy to see that it's more expensive and slower to search public records for each jurisdiction where the candidate has lived and traveled. And the farther back in time, the longer and more expensive it can be. But it's more accurate.

Going beyond aggregated data and public records checks leads to what many due diligence firms call Executive Background Checks or Full-Spectrum Due Diligence. These services can include a variety of data pulls and in-person investigative work, including social media analysis, interviewing references, confirming degrees, interviewing associates, colleagues, and neighbors. What can be done to examine a person's background is limited by law, money, and how much time you have to do the investigation.

The key when building your due diligence process is to begin by setting a strategy which meets your needs. Setting your strategy begins with understanding the trade-offs between speed, accuracy, and cost and deciding if a check-the-box process will meet your requirements. Most would reject a check-the-box program on principle, but we take a minute to address it here because for some companies, it actually is best. In highly regulated industries and in government contracting, particularly where some of your employees will need to hold U.S. Government security clearances, your due diligence process is already in place because you must comply with regulations. If your company is subject to regulation, the only question is whether there is a business case for doing more than the regulations require. In most cases, the regulations are comprehensive enough, and in some cases, expensive enough, that devoting even more resources to due diligence is not worthwhile. Consequently, heavily regulated companies don't need to do strategic planning beyond developing a system which efficiently implements the regulations which control due diligence for their industry.

For unregulated industry, the strategic planning process is more substantial. Once you understand the trade-offs, what's next? How do you build a cost-effective due diligence program which gives you what you need? It actually begins with deciding what harm your employees can do to your company and to your business model. It's also important to recognize that the potential harm an employee can do varies with the employee role. The more access an employee has, the more harm they can do, and consequently, the deeper (and more expensive) your due diligence process should be. It's important to recognize due diligence is not a one-size-fits-all process. A warehouse employee can harm the company through theft and negligent operation of warehouse machinery, while a sales person can harm the business' reputation through inappropriate interaction with customers. And a systems administrator has the ability to compromise your entire way of doing business, everything from stealing intellectual property to disabling and shutting down your electronic systems. The due diligence issues for the warehouse employee can probably be adequately addressed with a data pull from a firm using a data aggregator. But the systems administrator should be examined in much more depth before being trusted with access to the core of the business.

Consequently, when you go through the process of establishing the capabilities and behaviors which correlate to success in the specific job role, it is also important to determine how a person in that job role could harm the company and build a due diligence process that will collect data which correlates to the risk of a person engaging in that behavior. On the simple end of the scale, it is the very basic notions of honesty: who will lie, cheat, or steal, and who won't. On the complex end are deeper behavioral assessments which correlate to deeper security issues including insider threat, theft of trade secrets, and economic espionage.

On the simple end, it's simple: past behavior is the best predictor of future behavior. The most basic way to identify those who are likely to lie, cheat, and steal is to do criminal records checks, financial records checks (bankruptcy, small claims, and other financial disputes), and degree verification. Often, these simple records will reveal whether a person is honest, or whether, when under pressure, resorts to self-interest at the expense of others. And while we're still on simple things, it's important to notify candidates of what records will be checked and what indicators you're looking for. If you disqualify a candidate without having notified them before the records pull, they may have a legal remedy. The key is simple: build your due diligence process to correlate to the behaviors you are seeking and notify all candidates in advance, so nobody is surprised. Your goal is to identify and hire the people you need, not play "gotcha" with candidates who have taken the time to apply for work at your company.

For the complex end, a single data pull is not enough. You need to develop expertise in behavioral trait analysis or bring in expert assistance. To determine if a candidate poses an insider threat risk, you need to know what the threat is and what the indicators are—the "flags." And this requires expertise to ensure the flags you designate actually correlate to the risk you want to prevent.

At this point, it should be clear that a layered and dynamic process is required for effective due diligence. For some roles, a simple and quick records check process is all that is necessary to determine honesty. For roles with deeper access and correspondingly greater ability to cause harm, a records check is just the first step in a much deeper and more comprehensive review of a person's past behavior and may include predictive analytics to determine if a candidate is suitable for a high-trust position. With this understanding, your due diligence program will develop layers, with the simple and inexpensive work being done earlier in the process and the deeper, more complex data pulls and analysis being done toward the end. In fact, some of the deeper work is actually done after hiring and will become part of your insider threat program.

One of the keys to remember with due diligence is that we are dealing with people, and people change. Your assessment is only as good as your data, and as a person changes, the data changes with them, but the data lags. Consequently, while your initial hiring due diligence process can often be done with one data pull, and your deeper reviews are done with more comprehensive data, ongoing security requires periodic updated data and analysis to monitor how the threat changes in relation to how people change.

In addition, and even though it's outside our discussion of hiring due diligence, you should recognize that due diligence in hiring informs your ongoing security programs, including how often and how comprehensively you conduct reinvestigations. Your reinvestigations cycle not only is an important part of regulatory compliance, it also informs your insider threat and theft of trade secrets program. And these programs drive the effectiveness of your security and cybersecurity systems. Finally, your overall security programs depend on the effectiveness of your hiring and onboarding due diligence programs. It all interlocks.

And recognizing it all interlocks gives you the final and most significant advantage: creating and maintaining a continuous and ongoing security program means you actually don't need to build a perfect due diligence program for hiring. Since no static program will be effective to keep you safe, you don't need an onboarding system which weeds out one hundred percent of the bad apples. But you do need an ongoing process which continuously looks for problems and weeds them out as they appear. If each step in the security program cycle filters, refines, identifies, and removes threats, no one component of the cycle needs to be perfect—the system will be. So don't even try to build a due diligence hiring program which operates as a static barrier. Create a unified security cycle which includes due diligence, compliance, network security, insider threat, theft of trade secrets, and durable cybersecurity programs which interlock and support each other. As you can see, *Trust* is both complex and ongoing, and does not end at hiring. *Trust* is a crucial component of your company's culture, its way of being, and how it interacts both internally and externally.

Will They Do It?

When executed correctly, *Trust* will drive most of your internal security programs. Fundamentally, it's a choice; it's each individual's willingness to behave with shared intention. And so we come to *Will*. How do you tell which of the candidates that have met the *Can* and *Trust* standards are willing to function in the teams you have built to execute your company's purpose? Bill Bender articulates the starting point this way:

> **Bill:** The theory goes—and I subscribe to it—that it's the creativity and the ingenuity, and the innovative spirit of a human individual and those inherent personality traits that are likely to be the things that will make you a better cyber operator. And it's not all about just walking in the door with the technical skills and the geek science and engineering training, but it's instead, some of the soft skills that you would bring in terms of ingenuity, innovation, creativity, and the like.[14]

We think these "soft skills" are actually foundational skills, and they lead to the core of the person—the individual's behavioral characteristics—and the recognition that while behaviors are choices, they can be identified and evaluated before a hiring decision is made through the behavioral interview. And it is only behavioral characteristics as extracted through a behavioral interview which can offer a window into how an individual will act in the future. *Will* is a phase of the hiring process that generally does not receive the attention and weight that it should; our model hopes to change that. As Jason Meszaros,[15] the Director of Technology Infrastructure and Information Security for the Minnesota Twins Major League Baseball Team, explains:

> **Jason:** I sat on a panel at one of the local universities where it was all cybersecurity professionals, CISOs, etc. We sat down with all of the professors in charge of putting together cybersecurity programs. Every single one of them was highly focused on computer forensic experts, people who can dig into code, who can do that

---

[14] B. Bender, in discussion with the authors. July 08, 2020.

[15] Jason Meszaros came to the Minnesota Twins after serving in the United States Army for fifteen years, where he achieved the rank of Captain and spent the majority of his time in the Special Operations community as a human intelligence collector.

really deep dive. And of all the people in the panel, I was the only one who raised my hand and I said, "What about communication skills? What about problem solving skills?" They were so focused on, "We need to have the most highly technical people hitting the marketplace, because those are the ones who are going to get hired." The reality is, in my opinion (and I was the anomaly on the panel), that those are all great skills, and they need to know that information. But do they need to be so deep into it that they lose all the other skills? That's a huge negative in my opinion. I want people who can actually come in and communicate and articulate what the issue is, and how they're going to resolve it. That doesn't necessarily mean it's always technical, because not all problems that you solve are uber-technical problems, some of them are people issues. People make mistakes—people open the wrong link—and we have to resolve that and make sure that if they click ransomware, they know how to react, who to call. There's a whole process: a procedural focus, there's absolutely a communication focus, on all of those different skills in order to be successful and it's not just, "Can I dig deep into the code to figure out what the issue was?" You need those people in your office too, but there are additional skills that are out there.[16]

Unfortunately, many companies still don't appreciate the significance and impact of behavioral interviews—just as Jason was the anomaly on his panel. Upon accepting behavioral interviews as necessary, the key to successfully extracting differential data in the *Will* phase is to also accept that behaviors are job specific. There is no universal set of behaviors that a cybersecurity or IT person needs. However, there is a place to start.

If you have a job opening, then someone in your organization may already be doing that work. He may not be doing it well; he may be multi-hatted and overwhelmed; he may be on a termination trajectory; but someone is already doing the job. You may have had several people in the role over the previous months or even years. That's your data. And

---

[16] J. Meszaros, in discussion with the authors. August 03, 2020.

it's individualized to the company, the hiring manager, and the job role. Look at what made each previous person successful and what made them fail. Build a "perfect person" by reviewing these behavior characteristics with everyone who interacts with that role and who relies on the role—both external customers and internal information users. These data build the person you're looking for. And it's based on what you actually need.

And it is crucial to remember that what a person can do bears little relation to what they'll actually do, particularly under stress. In addition, choosing to engage in a behavior that you can do, but you don't like to do, is really where the rubber meets the road during the *Will* phase because stress tends to cause intermittent behaviors. When things are going well, the choice to behave in ways you don't prefer is easier. But when you're under stress, you're going to default to what you prefer, and that can result in disruptive behavior at the most stressful time. Consequently, the behavioral interview must be carefully structured to extract behavioral characteristics across a variety of circumstances—it becomes much more sophisticated when differentiating for crisis. You actually need to know if your candidate who can "speak people," and will do so when things are calm, will default to their preference when stressed, which is yelling a string of words that nobody understands and then watching the building burn because no one understood what they said. As Wheeler Coleman,[17] formerly the Senior Vice President and CIO of Blue Cross Blue Shield of Michigan and now the CEO of Executive Consultants United, explains:

> **Wheeler:** I am interested in learning about critical times in their work experiences. If we can get real examples from these individuals about how they addressed a crisis situation, we can find out how they're going to behave in tough times. It's easy to be cool, calm and collected when things are going well. But when the proverbial crap hits the fan, are they able to remain calm or do

---

[17] With more than thirty years of IT experience, Wheeler Coleman was most recently the Senior Vice President and CIO of Blue Cross Blue Shield of Michigan, where he was responsible for an IT budget in the hundreds of millions, and more than 2,000 resources (employees and contractors). Upon retiring, he became the CEO of Executive Consultants United, which offers IT consulting.

they freeze up? How do they treat others when problems arise? It's important to understand their behaviors.[18]

A final thought about the behavioral interview itself. Whether a person "interviews well" doesn't matter. But it doesn't matter for a very specific reason. It doesn't matter because it doesn't correlate to job performance. In other words, whether a person interviews well or poorly doesn't reveal whether they will do well or poorly on the job. You can have the best questions supported by brilliant validation and a perfect setting and still make poor hiring selections. The behavioral interview process is not about textbook answers to good questions. Good questions are just tools to extract the information you need. If you don't use them correctly, you'll still hire the wrong people. It's like having the best car and the worst driver—at best, you'll lose the race, at worst, you'll crash. It's not just about hearing a good answer. Because hearing a "good" answer takes you back down the "I like you because you're like me" dead end. Evaluating the behavioral interview is about understanding what the answer reveals. Most interviewers can't articulate the reasons why they think a particular answer is "good." This is because they don't understand what information the answer reveals. The key remains: use the behavioral interview to extract differential data relevant to the behavioral characteristics you need for the job role. Evaluating answers is not binary (i.e., "good" or "bad"). Correct evaluation produces differential data relevant to Success, Failure–Coachable, or Failure–Noncoachable. And the hiring decision is not binary either (i.e., "hire" or "don't hire"). It is Hire (standard onboarding), Hire (standard onboarding with focused coaching), or Don't Hire.

Getting Started

A few final thoughts to consider as you work your way through this process for the first time: first, this should be done for each job you hire for because each job has different success/failure behaviors, even if several jobs have the same hard skill, certification, and training requirements. The good news is, once you have worked through the success/failure process

---

[18] W. Coleman, in discussion with the authors. August 12, 2020.

a few times, you'll get the hang of it and it becomes easier. Second, by using this process, you'll begin considering candidates you would have rejected previously, and you'll reject those you would have considered to be ideal. This is unsettling at first, but the point is important: If you want a diverse, inclusive, and highly effective workforce with high employee retention and low turnover, you must hire the people who make you feel uncomfortable and who meet your *Can–Trust–Will* filters. You must get comfortable being uncomfortable.

There are two other factors to be aware of as you begin building job-specific descriptions. First, stay away from category-based presumptions: things like "older people are reliable," or "millennials are selfish." Fundamentally, these presumptions may be correct, but they simply aren't useful when building job descriptions. Why? Because you're not hiring a class of people, you're looking for a person. Millennials might be selfish, but the actual person who submitted an application may not be. Older people might be reliable, but the actual candidate who submitted a resumé might be a flake. Avoid building these presumptions into the job description and focus on describing what you need. Second, recognize that you may have a job which requires one or several personality traits which most people consider to be negative. It's counterintuitive, but very important—and we explore it in depth in Chapter 5.

Keeping all of this in mind, begin working through the specific job role, and categorize the behaviors of previous employees (all previous employees, not just the successful ones).

1. What are the required technical skills?
2. What are the required certifications?
3. What is the required training?
4. Which behaviors lead to success?
5. Which behaviors lead to failure?

The next step is to do a deep dive into item numbers three and five. Break training down into work which absolutely must be done before hiring and work which can be (not must be) done after hiring. Training then becomes an incentive rather than just a requirement.

Next analyze the failure behaviors. Separate these behaviors into what can be taught and what cannot be taught. In general, skills can be taught, but attitude can't, (i.e., you can teach most people how to drive a forklift safely, but you probably can't teach someone to be on time). Behaviors which can be taught go on the Failure–Coachable list, and those which can't be taught go on the Failure–Noncoachable list.

CHAPTER 3

Finding the Right Candidates

Both triple-threat movie stars and cybersecurity employees need the "it" factor. It can be a daunting process to find your next box office hit. Andrea developed a strategy for developing the initial talent pool involving multiple pathways:

> **Andrea:** If I have an open role, I'll reach out to search placement firms most certainly—there are amazing partners there and they have found me some great candidates. I work with some placement firms that know me and what I expect from a member of my staff, because what I look for is the whole package. So they might have the technical chops and amazing skills from that standpoint, but if they're missing any of the key important soft skills then they're probably not going to be a fit. I talk about expectations: they can be brilliant on the technical side, but I also need them to be able to speak to our attorneys and to walk the floor and to have that conversation and to understand our business. But even more importantly, I'll reach out to my network and see if they know anyone they can refer to me, and I've found some amazing talent that way. The most important insight is the insight of that from my peer colleagues at other firms, or within the industry.[1]

She speaks to the technical skills and the behavioral requirements, and how different candidate streams produce results. On one hand, search placement firms (recruiters) need to "know" her and what she expects from her employees. On the other hand, her network offers "insight and input" that is beyond reproach. These systems can function side-by-side,

---

[1] A. Markstrom, in discussion with the authors. June 24, 2020.

but building the initial candidate pool is difficult and takes hard work. Adam Lee describes it this way:

> **Adam:** Our recruiters do their best to find candidates via LinkedIn, various job boards, career fairs, a SANS pipeline, veterans groups and personal relationships. We have not found the magic pipeline yet. There are simply not enough GOOD cyber folks out there to fill all of our needs.

The "magic pipeline" may be the combination of pipelines. Michael Woodson underscores the way cybersecurity executives need to be integrally involved in the process of finding candidates:

> **Michael:** You have to think outside the box. HR will post a job, and that's kind of old school. I've had to be proactive. When I have an open position I have to go shop, I have to go out to the market. They're not equipped to do what they should be doing, and that's been my problem. A generic HR recruiter will not be able to find candidates. You need to have technical knowledge and be proactive. You can't just post the job and they will come.[2]

Wheeler Coleman furthers this perspective, advocating for cybersecurity leadership to actively dig into the prospective talent pools:

> **Wheeler:** Whenever I attend conferences, I look forward to the sessions, but I really like to interact with other attendees. I collect many cards, always scouting out talent. Recognizing that there are many people in the security world with talent, I go a step further to conduct behind the scene investigations to find out the reputation of leaders that trigger my interest.[3]

There are a few keys to the development of an initial cybersecurity talent pool, and our experts above each use them in different ways. First,

---

[2] M. Woodson, in discussion with the authors. July 20, 2020.

[3] W. Coleman, in discussion with the authors. August 12, 2020.

cybersecurity leadership—whether that's the CIO, CISO, CSO, or other executive—must be outwardly facing, and involved in the tight knit cybersecurity community. Going to conferences inherently includes the educational aspect, but it importantly includes the networking aspect; leaders should know what is happening in their field, both content-wise and talent-wise. This allows the corporate leaders to ensure that their company culture, vision, and mission are known to potentially interested talent pools, while at the same time seeing what those interested talent pools actually are.

Do You Know What You Want?

Shockingly, some companies may not know who they're looking for—despite having full and active job postings and "We're Hiring!" campaigns. Sometimes, completely new skills are necessary, behaviors and talents specific to what your organization is doing—whether that's migrating to the cloud, building an in-house SOC, or transitioning to new authentication measures. Importantly, due to the evolving nature of cybersecurity, every organization must take a deep dive into what their needs really are. Nick Davis explains how the field has changed and continues to change:

> **Nick:** The work has changed in the past twenty years. It used to be extremely technical in nature. That was the person who was responsible for engineering, architecting, building out, and then day-to-day operational management of information security-related technologies and infrastructure. What that has changed to (and is accelerating now), is that because of the prevalence of cloud service, we're looking more for people who are able to analyze information security controls, or are able to ask questions about compliance and regulation and governance, and understand how things are built and configured in the standards that they need, rather than actually have the hands-on expertise of running those applications and hardware themselves.[4]

---

[4] N. Davis, in discussion with the authors. July 27, 2020.

Frustratingly, companies that need to hire may not have the right tools to figure out who they're looking for. So they generally fall into the trap of The Big Mistake or banking on *Can* (without completing the process of *Trust–Will*). We focus on The Big Mistake in Chapter 4; without giving too much away just yet, this can occur when hiring parties either look for, or are given referrals to, candidates that are "a good fit" or a "great person." On the other hand, focusing solely on *Can*, again either through the hiring party's own searching mechanisms or a referral, only looks at the candidate's technical skills. Both of these paths lead to random results. While any hires referred to you through someone you trust could succeed, they may be the opposite—and in the end, it's random and does not take into account who you truly need.

Spotlight: "We Just Can't Find Good Candidates"

The executive coaching session had just started and the client, the COO (Chief Operating Officer) of a big-city nonprofit, had launched quickly into a frustrated outburst. It seems they had a VP (Vice President) opening which remained unfilled after nearly a year of searching, headhunters, and interviews. During this time, the COO was struggling to do the VP job on top of his own job and was getting increasing levels of criticism for doing both poorly.

As we dug into the problem, it soon became obvious that there were two camps: one thought the salary should be raised, the other thought the best available candidate should be selected. And then there was the CEO who demanded to know, with a certain level of frustration, why a candidate able to deliver on the job requirements (ten out of ten) at the going market rate could not be found? They were stuck arguing and not getting anywhere.

Why should we pay more?
Why should we settle for less than we need?
Why can't we find good candidates?

Recruiters in the IT and cybersecurity sphere should be well-equipped to help employers understand the market, as it can be overwhelming.

Paul Casale,[5] Senior Vice President of Recruiting at Mitchell Martin, illustrates the widespread confusion, speaking almost directly to the spotlight mentioned earlier:

> **Paul:** When I'm talking to hiring managers, I'm transparent with them. I may say the things you're asking for at this rate probably are not going to happen. Are you willing to be flexible on your wish list? They may have a laundry list of skills and experience that they want. When we read the description we may find their price point is lower than what we might be seeing in the market. We may be only able to find three or four of those skills at that rate. Part of our job is market education, especially in the cyber security space. I talked to a manager recently, for the first time, who had an opening that was cybersecurity related and it also had infrastructure and networking components to it. The role was open for eight months. I said you might have to ease up your requirements to find the right person or come up on the rate to get everything you need. And how vital of a need is this if it's been open this long?[6]

Sound familiar? Particularly in today's cybersecurity hiring market, as employment rates are high and skill levels are low, jobs stay open for too long and frustration continues to build. According to CyberSeek,[7] a project supported by NICE that focuses on supply and demand in the U.S. cybersecurity job market, there were approximately half a million open cybersecurity job listings from June 2019 through May 2020.[8]

---

[5] Paul Casale has over fifteen years of experience in IT staffing, and is currently the Senior Vice President of Recruiting, managing a team of over eighteen recruiters at Mitchell Martin, a national IT staffing and recruiting service provider.

[6] P. Casale, in discussion with the authors. June 26, 2020.

[7] CyberSeek, *About This Tool.* www.cyberseek.org/index.html#about

[8] CyberSeek, *Cybersecurity Supply/Demand Heat Map.* www.cyberseek.org/heatmap.html

Job Description

The solution is to begin at the beginning: by clearly establishing what you actually need. If you don't know what you need, you can't look for it. And even worse, you won't recognize what you need in the event you happen to stumble across it by chance. "But," you reply, "we know what we need—we have a job description." And that's where the problems begin. Take a look at your job description. Who wrote it? How old is it? When was it last updated? What does it include?

Well-defined job roles and responsibilities (including both technical and behavioral aspects) set you up for hiring success. Bill Brennan explains the significance of first defining exactly what you need:

> **Bill:** For any company, small or large, it's about defining what you actually need. We found over time that you might need someone who can run vulnerability scans, or I may need someone who can do computer network defense, or I may need someone who understands how to do security engineering, or I may need someone who understands how to do workforce development. Really understanding what you mean when you say I need a cyber person, whether that's going to the NICE model or defining it for yourself, massively increases your ability to not only work within your own recruitment, but also search for the folks that have the skills you need.[9]

The process will vary depending on the entity hiring, as Bill highlights. It follows that clear descriptions of job roles and responsibilities should aid in recruiting. The research shows that professionals in the field of cybersecurity respond better to clearly defined job requirements and descriptions. Lack of specificity is not only a "turn-off" to those with experience, it creates confusion for newbies.[10]

Job descriptions can be classified into one of three general categories:

---

[9] B. Brennan, in discussion with the authors. August 04, 2020.
[10] (ISC)², *Hiring and Retaining Top Cybersecurity Talent.* www.isc2.org/-/media/Files/Research/ISC2-Hiring-and-Retaining-Top-Cybersecurity-Talent.ashx (10)

1. The industry standard: This version can be developed internally or externally. Internally, it might come from an HR department or maybe from the department that has the vacancy. It might also come from an external expert, a consulting firm that sells research on industry trends, or a recruitment firm which offers job posting services in addition to talent acquisition. Regardless of where the industry standard version of a job description comes from, it generally has two deficits: first, the job competencies are so general they are meaningless, and second, the competencies are based on surveys, which only produce industry averages. The net result is a search for an average candidate which draws a candidate pool clustered around an average set of competencies driven by industry trends. Using an industry standard job description means you'll spend this year looking for a last year's average candidate. Both of which lead to problems.

2. The ideal candidate: This version can also be developed internally or externally, but it tries to solve the problems found in the industry standard description by going to the other extreme. The ideal candidate job description usually begins as an exercise—let's start by describing the perfect candidate and see who we get. This approach creates several problems, some of which were faced by the client company we met at the start of the chapter. First, the ideal candidate description is a fantasy. And since the existence of such a candidate has no connection with reality, such a candidate is never found.

3. The last person who had it: This version is most often found when decision makers want to get hiring done quickly. Surprisingly, as a strategy, it is not too far off the mark. Unfortunately, it often falls short because, to get done quickly, it's done thoughtlessly. What we often see is a list of certifications and skills which the last person had or which others in the department have, with no attention paid to critical behaviors that are also needed for a candidate to thrive and a work unit to succeed. This is another version of "let's see who we get" by quickly putting up a job description on a few job boards. The problem comes in sifting through responses because there are no candidate differentiators when the job description only includes specific skills and certifications.

Whether your job descriptions fall into one, or more than one, of these categories, once it is written, it may as well be set in stone. We beg you to write in pencil from now on.

Spotlight: Can, "Competency" and Certifications

Competency can be attained in many ways, especially related to cybersecurity. While it is largely dependent on the specific role and/or responsibility in question, competency may come from experience (work or personal), education (formal or self-taught), certifications, and training (either pre- or post-hire). Even though the intent at the outset is often to set the bar high, see who applies, and then compromise on one or a few competencies, the compromise often fails to emerge. This is because once a "good enough" candidate is identified, at least one person in the approval pipeline will ask why a candidate who fails to meet the job description is being considered at all. Rodney Petersen helpfully calls the problem of asking for everything plus the kitchen sink "over spec'ing":

> **Rodney:** Traditionally, the big three credentials to get a job are degrees, certifications, and experience, and everybody's looking for people with some combination of those three. Position descriptions are over-spec'ed, and the number of open jobs with certification requirements often exceed the number of people available who even hold them in the universe. So there's not enough people to fill those jobs.[11]

This problem is compounded in today's market, where the national average cybersecurity job supply–demand ratio is one to eight (versus the national average for all jobs, which is three to seven).[12] There are valuable cybersecurity candidates—whether for technical, compliance, risk, legal, or executive roles—that come from all different backgrounds.

Failing to capture talent pools without certain "buzzword" backgrounds is the problem our anecdotal COO client had with the CEO earlier in the

---

[11] R. Petersen, in discussion with the authors. July 28, 2020.
[12] CyberSeek, *Cybersecurity Supply/Demand Heat Map*. www.cyberseek.org/heatmap.html

chapter. The lesson is clear: if a competency is in the job description, very few hiring processes will permit a candidate without that competency to proceed. This is problematic on multiple levels: first, job descriptions for ideal candidates often include competencies which are not relevant to the job being performed. Most often this issue takes the form of requiring leadership ability of some type for individual contributor roles. Even in the cybersecurity world, not everyone needs to be, or should exhibit, leader behaviors when they are assigned to an individual contributor role. Individual contributors need to make individual contributions to the team they work on, but they do not need to lead the team. This could also include "ideal" or "mandatory" degrees, certifications and training, or decades of experience. But are they always necessary?

Some may quarrel with even posing this question. First, related to leadership: in a focused way, we agree that leadership is important, particularly when looking at business resilience processes and frontline leader development. Leader development is critical to any organization, and resilience requires the establishment of processes which identify leadership potential. However, that does not mean leadership ability should become a job competency for individual contributors. Individual contributors should be selected based on the ability to make an individual contribution. Those few who are identified as having leadership potential, which we address in later chapters, can and should, be brought into a leadership development pipeline. Second, related to education and experience, opinions are mixed. Rodney Petersen offers insight regarding knowledge and competencies:

> **Rodney:** Both degrees and certifications tend to test knowledge and memorization skills; the ability to take multiple choice, true/false tests, and that is not nearly as important as what you can do, how your skills can demonstrate your ability to apply the knowledge. We're moving the NICE Framework towards competencies because we think that's a better way for learners to demonstrate their accomplishments or what they can accomplish with the kind of competencies they both acquire and have the capacity to continue to acquire over time.[13]

---

[13] R. Petersen, in discussion with the authors. July 28, 2020.

Austin Berglas,[14] the Global Head of Professional Services for BlueVoyant, explains his thought process in hiring college grads without typical backgrounds or certifications to entry-level positions:

> **Austin:** I have a penetration tester who leads my penetration testing team, a former NSA cyber operations specialist—and that is where, underneath these guys and gals—these directors—is where I'm able to take that college graduate who has spent his high school time basically hacking boxes in his basement and getting up to speed, really growing a passion for understanding vulnerability. I'll hire that person—number one is they want to learn, they want to grow, and they're affordable.[15]

What does the college graduate who has spent his high school years passionately hacking boxes in his basement demonstrate? He may not have the standard understanding of the requisite tools or software. But behaviorally, he is a learner. We can break it down with an analogy in a completely different field: cargo pilots versus test pilots. Generally, flying cargo is very simple—you go from point A to point B and back from point B to point A. If you're a test pilot, your job is to actively put yourself in situations where you need to quickly and accurately solve problems. Test pilots are learners, just as hackers can be learners. This behavior can be uncovered with correlating behavioral question sets during the *Will* phase.

In cybersecurity, we hear more and more stories about hiring managers finding the ideal candidate—but having trouble dealing with an organizational response to that candidate's missing fill-in-the-blank formal education requirement. Michael Woodson still remembers the "one that got away":

---

[14] Austin Berglas is the Global Head of Professional Services for BlueVoyant, a cybersecurity provider. He previously served twenty-two years in the U.S. Government as both an FBI Special Agent and head of all cyber investigations in New York City, and as an Officer in the U.S. Army.

[15] A. Berglas, in discussion with the authors. June 30, 2020.

Michael: Sometimes you miss a good candidate because he or she didn't finish the degree. I have found an individual like that. However, he didn't have a degree, and the requirement was for a degree. So that put him out of the loop. We had to take a look at that, and it was hard for people to understand that this guy has everything we've been looking for—but he didn't have the degree. His was one of the best interviews. But I couldn't hire him. They wouldn't allow me. He was going to be my report, my deputy, and I couldn't hire the guy.[16]

Good candidates, sometimes the very best individual contributors or go-to employees, will be overlooked if the ideal job description requires behaviors and abilities which are great to have, but do not correlate to successful performance of the job described.

But there are significant ways in which formal education, certificates, and training can truly make a difference. Most obviously, the knowledge gained can be a game-changer, and many of the requisite degree and certificate requirements we see in cybersecurity job descriptions make sense based on the defined responsibilities. It may depend on how mature the company's cybersecurity team is, it may depend on how senior the role is, and it may depend on what the particulars of the job are. Nick points out that companies without mature cybersecurity teams tend to be looking for people early in their careers:

Nick: They're looking for someone who's eager to take on work across multiple areas of search, a jack-of-all-trades in information security. And they're looking to hire people at the entry level, rather than at the seasoned level because they know that a person they hire at the entry level can take them from zero to fifty percent which is a lot better than where they were. It's only when you have a very mature information security program that companies are interested in hiring people that have experience in working in some other organizations. Since the company is immature, they're

---

[16] M. Woodson, in discussion with the authors. July 20, 2020.

basically looking for a warm body that can do basic work. They're usually looking for individuals that can do five or six different things relative to information security, who can be the go-to person for information security. But they're not looking for specialists, they're not looking for people to join a team already in place.[17]

Formal education certainly points to behaviors that correlate to success as well, and Nick's analysis of when and why to hire recent grads highlights why these newly formally anointed cybersecurity professionals can be a serious asset. John Kolb,[18] the Vice President for Information Services and Technology and CIO of Rensselaer Polytechnic Institute, explains what degrees demonstrate to him:

> **John:** I actually think the credentials, a lot of times, is what gets you in the door. And to me, what it typically says is that you're disciplined enough to make it through the course/curriculum, and you're able to stay up with the work, learn a new subject, pass the assessments and so on. And that's useful, because you want somebody who's disciplined—you don't necessarily just want the smartest person in the room. You want somebody who's going to be disciplined about how and what their approach is, and how they're going about things. You might find the unicorn, the smartest person in the room that didn't go to school and so on—and that's okay. But I think the degree is important for me. It says that somebody applied themselves and came out the other side. One of the most important personal traits is persistence. A lot of these problems don't get solved in minutes or days or weeks, even—they take some time to really think through and test and so on.[19]

---

[17] N. Davis, in discussion with the authors. July 27, 2020.

[18] John Kolb has worked with Rensselaer Polytechnic Institute for over thirty years; he currently is the Vice President for Information Services and Technology and CIO, and previously served as the Dean of Computing and Information Services, amongst other leadership roles.

[19] J. Kolb, in discussion with the authors. July 28, 2020.

The behaviors John describes—discipline and persistence—are essential to many cybersecurity job roles. As Adam Bricker,[20] the founding Executive Director of the Carolina Cyber Center, explains, the Carolina Cyber Center aims to integrate "essential life skills" into a student's cybersecurity professional development program:

> **Adam:** Our goal is not to just get you the interview (e.g., with certifications and experience), or simply to get you the job (e.g., by adding in professional skills like interviewing and speaking). Our superordinate goal is to prepare you for a successful career to serve our nation, and we do so by integrating the development of one's essential life skills such as discipline, creativity, collaboration and grit. We can all differentiate between "just a job" and a "profession." Professionals should have a growth mindset.[21]

Adam is describing behaviors that correlate to success for many cybersecurity professionals. Attempting to describe this concept reminds us of the great, but relatively unknown mountaineer, Dr. Thomas Hornbein who, with Willi Unsoeld in 1963, made the first ascent of the West Ridge of Mount Everest, and by descending the Southeast ridge, made the first known traverse of Everest. When asked why he climbed such dangerous mountains, he did not repeat George Mallory's "because it's there" answer. Dr. Hornbein, an anesthesiologist and Professor at the University of Washington Medical School, said that he climbed because it was such a deep part of who and what he was as a person, that not climbing was not an option. That's the depth of character you need to look for when assessing Adam's "essential life skills."

Students, nonpros, and transitioning candidates may demonstrate these essential life skills—the behaviors that correlate to success in cybersecurity job roles. Still, regardless of all experience, employers tend to

---

[20] Adam Bricker began his career as an aerospace engineer. He has worked as a Director of Information Systems, CIO, and founder of EdTech, medical informatics, SaaS software and product development companies, and became the founding Executive Director of the Carolina Cyber Center in January 2020.

[21] A. Bricker, in discussion with the authors. July 13, 2020.

request many of the four-letter certification abbreviations on candidates' resumés. As Paul has seen from some of his clients:

> **Paul:** A lot of times you'll see requirements, and it'll say, "We require 1,700 certifications in cybersecurity."[22]

Fortunately, certifications may be acquired by the right candidate, post-hire. There are a variety of organizations that offer certifications related to cybersecurity, and some are more well-respected and well-utilized than others. The well-known certifications include offerings from nonprofit and for-profit organizations, ranging from information systems security, to cloud security, to privacy, to ethical hacking, to digital forensics work. There are many levels of certs, all geared toward different aspects of cybersecurity. New certifications, whether based on new technologies or new vulnerabilities, crop up every year. In a recent survey which was skewed toward defining cybersecurity professionals as more technically skilled,[23] eighty-one percent of respondents anticipated that they would need to obtain additional certifications or training in their preparation for future roles.[24] More generally, eighty-four percent of respondents took the position that they were planning to pursue a new cybersecurity-related certification at some point, as employees and candidates look to working toward certifications to improve or add to their skill sets, to stay competitive, and to advance or develop their careers.[25]

There are many certificate options to demonstrate increased education, skill, and ability—each at differing levels (beginner, career advancement, and specialty). But there may be a catch in hiring someone just for the certifications, as Austin explains:

---

[22] P. Casale, in discussion with the authors. June 26, 2020.

[23] Specifically defining "cybersecurity professionals" as ". . .a mix of certified professionals in official cybersecurity functions as well as IT/ICT professionals who spend at least twenty-five percent of a typical work week handling responsibilities specifically related to cybersecurity." (ISC)², *2019 Cybersecurity Workforce Study.* www.isc2.org/-/media/ISC2/Research/2019-Cybersecurity-Workforce-Study/ISC2-Cybersecurity-Workforce-Study-2019.ashx (4)

[24] *Id.* at 30.

[25] *Id.* at 31–32.

Austin: When you spend thousands of dollars and hours on those certifications, that time can be spent toward actually having hands on data, actually ripping apart hard drives and actually doing penetration testing, and learning. Because what you read in the book, if you've ever gotten one of these certifications, what you read in the book is really just learning the page. It's not that way in reality; I want to hire somebody who has done penetration testing, has developed their own skill set, understands the tools, understands how to get around things that you can't find in a book. That's what I'm looking for. And if a client wants to hire us and needs a certain certification, and we don't have it—it's very simple for me to send one of my people to study for an online certification for a couple weeks and get it.[26]

Inherent in what Austin is saying is that "book learning" needs to be balanced by experience—whether that's on-the-job, in school, or in one's basement, And the candidate needs to be able to, and want to, learn. Andrea points out that leaders must be willing to invest in their team:

Andrea: My role is to invest in my team and get them "skilled up" or "leveled up" with new skills, be it training, or going to attend conferences where they've not had that exposure before, but most importantly understanding what are the new skill sets that are going to be critical so that we can grow as a thriving IT organization.[27]

So, some aspects of competence may come post-hire, whether they are foundational or expansive. The key is to know what the necessities are for your job description. Creating a functional, rational, and evolutionary job description begins with understanding that each job in your company needs its own job description. Some jobs may be fairly close, but each role must have its own, focused summary of requirements. First, use what you already know. If this is an existing job, analyze prior

---

[26] A. Berglas, in discussion with the authors. June 30, 2020.
[27] M. Andrea, in discussion with the authors. June 24, 2020.

performance in the specific job role. If this is a newly created job that is being filled for the first time, review the growth that has occurred within your organization, recognizing that the person currently performing related job tasks cannot meet demand, and/or an audit has revealed new necessities.

Good candidate pools come from clear and focused job descriptions which are relevant to what you actually need in your business. Industry trends, ideal candidate descriptions, and "throw it against the wall to see what sticks" do not draw in the candidates you need. Without a properly formed candidate pool, nothing you do in a selection process or in an interview phase matters. It's the job description which drives the candidate pool, and the candidate pool provides the foundation for finding the employee you need. These complex and difficult trade-offs are exactly why capability, skill, training, and certification are placed at the very top of the process in the *Can* phase. By being first, these most difficult trade-offs can be made before time and resources are spent by both employers and candidates on other parts of the hiring process. While different companies will work through these trade-offs in very different ways as they set up their testing programs and identify their certification requirements, there is one issue all companies will have in the hiring process: Where do you find candidates?

This is not about finding "good" candidates or "high-quality" candidates. Remember, the hiring model will produce that outcome if properly structured and operated. Regardless, any process needs candidates, people interested in working for the company and willing to apply for the job. What happens when you have a great process, focused testing, the right certifications identified, but nobody applies? Or (and more common) most of your applicants simply don't meet the basic capability requirements. What then? Debate usually ensues. The standard approaches are either to attempt to restructure the job requirements so more applicants will have the necessary skill (dumbing down) or to raise the offered salary. Neither works. Unless you need a person with truly unique capabilities, the problem isn't the requirements. And if the salary is within five percent of market rates, it's not the salary. The key is to find out what the cause is, and the solution is to go to the source. Where do your prospective candidates come from?

Where you look depends on what you need. And how you create a steady stream of candidates depends on where you look.

For Entry Level, Go to School

The most important thing any company of any size can do to ensure its cybersecurity hiring funnel remains full is to establish and maintain relationships with schools to offer cybersecurity training, certifications, or internships. This does not mean having a booth at the job fair each year. It does not mean offering tours to the graduating class, and it does not mean making a donation to the annual auction. You must build an ongoing values-based relationship with the school and with the students as they are coming through the program. Not all of them will be interested in your company, not all of them will want to stay in town when they are done with school. But some will. And the key is to make it easy for them to get to know you and for you to get to know them. Offer to be a guest lecturer on whatever your specialty is. Be an adjunct professor if they need one. Get involved in the mentoring program. If they don't have one, find out why. Alexi Michaels details her experience in the job market directly after college:

> **Alexi:** My current boss said I was part of a very competitive applicant pool. But since starting at BlackBag, I have already contributed so many new suggestions to make programs better—which no one has yet brought to the table. And I think that is because, as a "newer" examiner, I have different views on examinations compared to the senior examiner who has been doing investigations the same way with the same tools for as long as he or she can remember. Now a lot of people rely on their tools to find the answers for them, and in my college courses we didn't just learn about how to use the top tools, but we learned how to do an investigation without the tools. Undergrads study and are heads down in their textbooks learning about digital forensics and the information is fresh in their brains when graduating. I think companies should 100% take advantage of this![28]

---

[28] A. Michaels, in discussion with the authors. July 03, 2020.

Alexi's first job after college was actually related to an internship she had with the same company. Remember, the key to a strong team is relationships which are built on communication and trust. Building relationships takes time, and one can never predict which relationships will be productive and which will be short-lived. The key is to position your company to have as many relationships as possible with the pool of people who are working toward the education and experience you need in your company. You'll learn about your candidate pool long before you need to make a hiring decision. And with more data, you'll make a better decision. Does the CEO need to go? It depends. If you have a five-person firm, everyone should participate. If your company is very large, then the most senior person who works at the location should be involved. If you send last year's new hire to mentor their friends who are graduating this year, you lack legitimacy. Share your time and expertise, and serendipity will work in your favor.

For Laterals, Go to Your Networks

Some are leery about poaching talent from other companies. Others are only concerned about being caught poaching talent. The reality is, employees move through the market and companies' needs change over time. The key here is to be in the market in order to understand what everyone is doing, to reiterate the tactics discussed in the beginning of this chapter. As Stewart Gibson explains:

> **Stewart:** The initial job requirement I presented to our recruiters was that I was looking for a direct report to a CISO that wants to make that next step and become a CISO. Hard core coders did not seem to be able to demonstrate they could make that step, and so I did refine what I was looking for. I started looking for sitting CISOs who were already successful and liked their current position, but maybe did not like the commute, or wanted to be closer to family. They were willing to make a move but not because they were not happy in their position. I did not want someone who was disgruntled with their current employer and was just itching to get out.[29]

---

[29] S. Gibson interview, July 27, 2020.

The knowledge Stewart mentions can be gained from building and knowing your network. The cybersecurity community is tight knit and, at times, competitive. The best way to attract the best talent is to set high standards and adhere to them and to treat everyone in your company well and make sure it is well known. There are ways to combat a competitive mentality when seeking out laterals externally. First, it's understanding that some people are happy where they are no matter what, and they are simply not going to move. But second: some people are happy where they are, while also having goals which cannot be met there (whether that's a promotion that can't happen because the company structure won't allow it, or the person in that slot is staying put). Those candidates can find growth by moving laterally to another company and then potentially transitioning back to their former employer at a higher level. Companies can find ways to make this mutually beneficial; it does not have to be a negative process. Orchestrating lateral movements properly can be a win–win.

For Laterals, Look Internally

The new cybersecurity workforce members you need may already be at your organization. Whether they have always been under the IT umbrella or have worked in a completely different line function (but know the business), internal employees may be a secret weapon. Amanda acknowledges how her internal career path from a management reporting analyst (where she reported to accounting, risk, and operations), to assisting the infosec team with developing incident response and business continuity plans, to officially starting in the infosec arena with a role as an information security analyst (focusing on governance, risk, and compliance):

> **Amanda:** Hiring a known entity from within the organization can reduce training time, even if the hire is outside of information security or information technology. An understanding of different business lines and knowing the organization is a crucial part of identifying unusual activity and potential threats.[30]

---

[30] A. Tilley, in discussion with the authors. July 02, 2020.

Amanda's employer acknowledged her talent, interest, and motivation—and allowed her to grow within the structure of the bank. Mid- to large-size businesses have an advantage in being able to seek out and develop a cybersecurity workforce (to an extent) from within. While IT professionals have the "solid foundation to contribute to an organization's cybersecurity practice," the shared responsibility across an organization, which is inherent in cybersecurity, means employees with transferable skills could be trained up as well. If they understand the inner workings of the business, know the way data flows in, out, and through, and/or are experienced in the existing risks (whether that's through legal or compliance), passionate, dedicated, and interested employees can be leveled up accordingly.[31]

Larger organizations may strive to put in place a similar proficiency assessment and mobility process that Leidos has perfected. Building on the concepts discussed in Chapter 1, and Bill Bender's explanation of the Leidos cybersecurity workforce program, Leidos' defined work roles and related *Can* assessments allow for ease of mobility within the organization. Bill continues:

> **Bill:** I think it's something on the order of 1,700 different sort of proficiency assessments that can take place over time for individuals. It allows us to have mobility within the organization as a result; this is a set of very sophisticated and measurable field aptitudes and experiences that lead to proficiency levels and the ability to move vertically and horizontally without always having the need for more training. There's a good alignment between what you do and the experience you've had and the proficiency you hold to this next job or set of jobs; it allows a lot of movement which is seen as a very positive thing. It's not the redundancy that comes with just one role for as long as you're willing to stick around, and that's proven to be very effective. I think, generally speaking, the proficiency levels have motivated people to stretch and to attain;

---

[31] (ISC)², *2019 Cybersecurity Workforce Study.* www.isc2.org/-/media/ISC2/Research/2019-Cybersecurity-Workforce-Study/ISC2-Cybersecurity-Workforce-Study-2019.ashx (35)

it becomes competitive in nature—and of course it's purely based on what they're able to attain and it's very clearly defined and measurable outcomes. And therefore, there's the self-motivation that takes over and they're compensated appropriately for those additional proficiency levels that they're able to attain. A lot of it is self-initiated, so that's a positive for us.[32]

Self-motivation among internal employees, and organized processes for vertical and horizontal mobility, mean valuable sources of cybersecurity hires already trained up on the business.

What About Jobs With High Turnover?

Many companies struggle with high turnover and ensuring you have a well-tuned hiring process and a steady stream of interested candidates entering your system can help. There is one key pitfall to avoid: don't presumé the solution is to stop the turnover.

This may seem counterintuitive, but it actually goes back to one of our initial rules: Don't try to solve a problem until you know the cause. Sometimes, high turnover is a symptom of a problem which needs to be addressed, and when fixed, the high turnover disappears. However, in some very specific situations, high turnover is not indicative of a problem; it's just part of the job. Many entry-level jobs have high turnover because they are entry level. Security guards may be gaining experience which qualifies them for law enforcement jobs, and retail employees may be learning the business to qualify for a management track.

If the nature of the job means that most employees stay, for example, two years, then it's a mistake to try creating incentives designed to keep people longer. Better outcomes can be obtained by planning for high turnover and facilitating the transition. Build relationships with schools or other companies who provide you candidates to ensure you have a steady supply. Help your soon-to-depart employees find the next step in their careers by maintaining connections with the companies who need their newly developed experience. The entry-level employee who you set

---

[32] B. Bender, in discussion with the authors. July 08, 2020.

on a development path may come back to you in a few years as a seasoned leader, capable of doing more than if she had stayed.

What happens if you discover that the type of person and the type of qualifications you're looking for simply can't be found in the area? Actually, that's valuable information. Even though it's frustrating, knowing there are not qualified candidates available in commute distance will drive necessary strategic changes in your business. This lets you know you have to draw candidates in based on geography, or figure out how you can leverage that skill remotely. The point remains: putting capability first is critical because it reveals and informs the rest of the process. The last thing you want is to keep looking for a person who simply doesn't exist where you are located.

Working With a Recruiter

Recruiter services can appear to be a miraculous fountain in a sandy desert. But recruiting firms are only valuable if they are properly utilized. If you choose to retain a recruiter, you must ensure that recruiter is more than just a mirage. Most importantly, you need to manage that recruiter—meaning, you must find a recruiter who is willing to be managed. Bob Keegan,[33] the Vice President of Cybersecurity Sales at Mitchell Martin, explains why the right recruiter needs to be a partner, both to listen and advise:

> **Bob:** We are not going to a client looking to get a requirement from them—we work together on requirements. We really want to go in from day one and truly be a partner. What I've seen in the cybersecurity market reminds me of way back when, when I was working a Lehman Brothers account. Lehman Brothers back in the early days used to promote people very quickly to managers, and they would be asked to make management decisions when they've never hired a person in their lives—they were in charge of writ-

---

[33] Bob Keegan started in the IT staffing business in 1990, in downtown New York City. Currently, Bob manages the cybersecurity niche at Mitchell Martin, with a national scope.

ing requirements. The same thing is happening in cybersecurity. People are being asked to take on roles inside cybersecurity groups within their organization, which they may not understand fully. So when they write requirements, they end up putting a laundry list of things together because they think that's what they really need. So we end up educating the client, many, many times, and hopefully we can get to it early in the process, but sometimes it takes a long time to get to help the client figure out what they really need to be effective to get the job done.[34]

Working with a recruiter requires skillful communication. In order to manage a recruiter, a few preliminary puzzle pieces must be in place: knowing what you are looking for, having a draft job description to work from, and understanding and establishing specific filters for the recruiters to use and quality checks to ensure you are getting what you have requested. Recruiters may push to simply take a job title from you and then sell their reputation to get the position filled ("We provide the best candidates in the industry," to "We have the best access to the best candidates," to "We know best"). But relying on a vendor to provide "the best" will most often not get you what you actually need. A good recruiter can get you a pool of applicants that fit your true needs and may proactively confirm background information before your team digs in. They may also help you with the other layers of the hiring process—especially if you have not hired in cybersecurity before, with guidance on what the market looks like, what employee concerns and requests are, and what turnover looks like in certain fields.

The Right (and Wrong) Way to Use a Resumé

There are countless books, seminars, and counseling services dedicated to helping job-seekers create, hone, and manage their resumés. But the same is not true for hiring managers and HR professionals. The teams sifting through and reading resumés need guidance as well, and the fundamental problem is that resumés, even good resumés, don't reveal that much.

---

[34] B. Keegan, in discussion with the authors. June 26, 2020.

Consequently, after you post a job, your intake process immediately gets overwhelmed by the volume of resumés which land on somebody's desk or computer.

Generally, the first step in reviewing resumés is to determine who meets the job requirements and who is aspirational. Often, a large percentage of applicants fail to meet the job requirements and are just hoping to impress somebody if they can just get an interview. This immediately causes a volume problem which Bill Thornton,[35] the Vice President Risk Management and Technology, Fraud and IT Security at Discover Financial Services, recalled the last time he posted a job and got seventy resumés in response:

> **Bill:** I don't have time to go through seventy resumés, so HR does that. Then, once they start feeding me resumés, I pick who I want a quick phone call with, and we'll do a quick phone screening which I will conduct if it's a direct hire for me.[36]

And in addition to the volume problem, there's a valid concern over accuracy. Do the resumés accurately recite the applicant's qualifications? Michael Woodson offers his opinion:

> **Michael:** So you know what you're looking for, they're going to give you a bunch of resumés. The reality is, how much truth is in that resumé? It's often that I find the very people that I'm looking for aren't the ones that have applied for that job.[37]

And for ultra-high volume postings, where there are keyword searches and even AI reviews, are the resumés being selected the best candidates,

---

[35] Bill Thornton has over twenty years of leadership experience that includes multiple C-level roles and the rank of Brigadier General in the United States Air Force. His current role is with Discover Financial Services, where he is the Vice President Risk Management and Technology, Fraud and IT Security.

[36] B. Thornton, in discussion with the authors. July 29, 2020.

[37] M. Woodson, in discussion with the authors. July 20, 2020.

or just the candidates who figured out which keywords to use? Paul Casale opens us up to the problem and the beginnings of the solution:

> **Paul:** My team has all the latest and greatest technology around to find the right people in the cyber space. We give our recruiters the tools they need to succeed but they are especially trained at digging down on the soft skills. We can find buzzwords on a resumé all day, but if we didn't really narrow down what they have done on the job and their personality in explaining it, then match it up to the hiring managers' requests, we wouldn't be as successful as we are. Our candidate pitches are tailor-made to what the manager is seeking when we find the right talent.[38]

This is a problem which has both practical and legal ramifications. Faced with a stack of applicants who all meet whatever the initial resumé review process is, how do you decide whom to interview? How do you treat everyone fairly?

The bottom line is actually simple: The resumé doesn't really give you much. Candidates spend a huge amount of time and effort to write resumés, and then put in ongoing effort to mold a unique version of the resumé to correspond to the job. We know because we've learned how and we've taught the techniques to many job-seekers. HR departments spend a good deal of time analyzing resumés to determine if there is a "match" between the candidate's background and the hiring manager's requirements. But in reality, other than a generic sense of "who should we interview" which is often driven by how close to the top of the stack a given resumé randomly appears, how resumés are written and how they are reviewed does not extract differential data regarding whether an applicant can or will do the job you need done. It's truly a waste of effort.

And after the initial review, what happens most often is a stack of resumés will land on the desk of a frontline manager with a verbal instruction to "hire the best three" or some other arbitrary number. This leads to a variety of problems ranging from hidden bias, to relying on feelings

---

[38] P. Casale, in discussion with the authors. June 26, 2020.

like "good fit," which seem relevant but are actually not indicative of high job performance. We have mentioned this before and will go into detail during Chapter 4's discussion about The Big Mistake. But with an essentially arbitrary approach, you not only fail to identify people who will succeed at your company, you become open to a host of legal issues ranging from failing to meet diversity and inclusion requirements to discriminatory hiring practices.

The good news is, when you use *Can–Trust–Will*, you don't need to look at resumés because all of the data you need to make the best possible hiring decision will be extracted during the process. Consequently, we strongly recommend chucking the old process of resumés and applications for your cybersecurity hiring program and building out a *Can–Trust–Will* process which identifies the technical skills and behavioral characteristics which correlate with success for each work role in your company.

However, for the intervening time, however long it might be, that you continue using a process which involves collecting and reviewing resumés, it is critical to analyze the resumé to answer just two questions. The first question is whether the resumé shows sufficient training or experience to conclude that the candidate has the technical skill to do the job. If so, the training and experience claimed should be quickly verified before the candidate moves forward. The second question is whether the resumé shows experience or other data which gives insight into the candidate's behavior characteristics. The final step is to decide, based on the totality of what you have extracted regarding the applicant's verified technical skill and potential behavior, whether to recommend the person be interviewed.

This process should seem faintly familiar because it's a resumé-review version of *Can–Trust–Will*. The sole purpose of this resumé review is to help you decide whom to interview. Plain and simple. And that's all the resumé should be used for. Hopefully, at this point, you'll have a number of objections to this resumé-review recommendation—it's imprecise, it's too shallow, I won't be able to tell who to interview. And you're right. But you're right for a very specific reason. By going through this process, you are clearly seeing how little you can learn about a person from a resumé. In addition, you are using a process which is sufficiently structured, so you can no longer hide behind imprecise evaluating phrases. No more "good fit for the team," "understands our culture," or "great resumé."

After resumés have been reviewed and interviews offered, the purpose of the resumé ends. The resumé should not guide interview questions, or even be present at the interview. The worst interviews are conducted by a person looking at the candidate's resumé and asking questions while working through the job history section. Such an interview reveals nothing about the candidate and gathers no differential data regarding whether the candidate fits the behaviors you need for the job vacancy you have. The interview should be used as a quest to gather behavioral data, per the final phase of our hiring model, *Will*—and using a resumé during the interview prevents you from doing so.

In fact, an interview centered around a resumé ("What was it like working at ABC Corporation?") results in a conversation that will leave you comfortable or uncomfortable—meaning, you either "like" the candidate or you don't. And, as illustrated earlier, we are likely to be comfortable with people who are like us and uncomfortable with people who are not. Resumé-based interviews, it follows, may actually be at the root of most diversity and inclusion problems. We will examine in depth how to conduct effective interviews in Chapter 6.

The only thing worse than a resumé-based interview is a resumé-based hiring decision. Candidates, if they are getting good advice, understand the resumé gets them the interview, not the job. The same advice applies to the hiring manager. The resumé, however impressive, should never be used as the basis for a job offer. For every one story of a successful hire off of a resumé only, there are perhaps hundreds of stories (which never get told) of failures. "Great" resumés simply don't correlate to job performance.

A Final Observation

If you've ever written a resumé, you know that it never tells the whole story of a candidate. Resumé writing is difficult principally because of the necessity to omit significant events and accomplishments due to space and relevance considerations. It never reveals the whole person. To make a good hiring decision you must know the whole person. Creating and operating the *Can–Trust–Will* process will ensure you know the whole person before you make a job offer. Getting derailed by a great resumé is always a mistake. Not just because you probably will hire someone who isn't what you need, and not just because that bad hiring decision is expensive. But mostly because your immediate decision to snatch up the great resumé—the shiny object which catches the eye—operates to pre-empt the truly great candidate who is in your interview pool but is never found because you sent them a "the position has been filled" message. They are right there, waiting to be a great part of your extraordinary team, and you missed them because you chanced across a good-looking resumé which just happened to be higher in the stack.

Interestingly, a similar theory applies to resumés that appear to show a lack of experience or relevant *Can* skills. Just as a stellar resumé will not reveal the entire person, a less-than-sparkling resumé doesn't tell the whole story either. Going back to our earlier discussion of hiring recent grads or candidates that need to be "trained up," these resumés may have a diamond-in-the-rough new hire hiding behind them. Amanda explains:

> **Amanda:** We just hired someone that if you just made a decision based solely on the resumé, the candidate probably wouldn't have made it to the video interview round; however, after getting to know the candidate through these multiple interview rounds, we found the perfect fit for our team. How the candidate conducted herself—calm under pressure, being able to speak eloquently, pre-sentation, and being able to explain technical concepts simply, set this candidate apart. We've also had candidates with perfect resumés, but in the end weren't up to par.[39]

The common error comes when reviewing a stack of resumés or inter-viewing candidates in groups—the natural tendency is to begin evalu-ating on the curve. The result is you interview the best candidates from the stack when you should only be interviewing the candidates you need. It might be all of them, it may be none of them, but the critical point remains: interviews should be given to candidates who are likely to be what you need—it's the first step away from the old confirmation mindset and toward the much more effective selection mindset.

---

[39] A. Tilley, in discussion with the authors. July 02, 2020.

CHAPTER 4

The Big Mistake
(and How to Avoid It)

The Double-Edged Sword of "Fitting In"

So you have the filters set: you have the job description, the due diligence measures to employ, and tests to proctor and review. But like any good relationship, we need that "spark." In the context of hiring the right candidate, that spark translates to the cherry-on-top of actually liking the new recruit. Arguably, we typically like people who are ... just like us. And such is The Big Mistake: hiring someone because he or she is like you. Just because someone is "just like me!" or "reminds me of myself!" or interviews well (because ... he or she is "so much like me") does not correlate to job performance.

Spotlight: The Nice Guy

When you're asked to picture someone who works in tech, the stereotypical image of a loner in a hoodie often comes to mind. But a company (who later became our client) lucked out: they had a cybersecurity systems architect who was funny, lively, and constantly smiling, come in to interview for a senior position work role. His interview went well as he charmed the boutique team and easily passed the knowledge, skills, and abilities (KSA) tests. He was hired and assigned the serious task of designing and auditing security structures to keep hackers out. Unfortunately, as a new hire, he quickly turned out to be a constant disruptor in the office, pulling people out of their workstations to tell stories, making jokes while struggling to get through routine tasks, and disappearing during stressful situations. How could this happen?

The bad hiring decision made by our client was caused by a progression of problems. And it begins by what we call being "influenced by personality." The candidate comes in and presents a personality full of high-impact charisma during the interview, and the interviewer's visceral response is to be impressed, and more significantly, the interviewer feels good. So the interviewer makes the mistake of evaluating the candidate solely based on the charismatic personality he presented. But they don't dig deeper. Why don't they dig deeper? How did they get fooled?

There are two forces at work which cause most hiring managers not to dig beyond what the candidate presents and get fooled as a consequence. The first force at work is, it's easy to feel good. In addition, it's a relief to feel good, particularly when interviewing job candidates. You've got to fill this position, interviewing is difficult, and here's a candidate who makes you feel good—great, we're done! Unfortunately, using the feel-good evaluation is essentially a decision about whether you like the candidate, but it's not an assessment of whether the person will be successful in the job role. And that leads to the second force at work when you allow yourself to be influenced by a good interview—jumping to conclusions, or more precisely: false correlation. You presume that a person you like—who is really a person like you—will succeed in the job role.

And that's the core of false correlation. It's a presumption without basis. When you feel good about a candidate, usually because you like them since they are "like you," you need to articulate reasons for your decision to hire. We have many ways to make this appear legitimate—"good fit" or "rockstar"—but they are all variations of "I feel good because he's like me." Fundamentally, it's lazy. You feel good about the person, so the interview is over, and the job is filled. But more deeply, it leads to uniformity, a shallow bench, and makes diversity and inclusion impossible. Why? Because you hire people who are like you.

In this case, the hiring manager was fooled by high-impact charisma during the interview. He presumed that the behavior shown during the interview process meant the candidate would be a successful employee for that company. He thought "fun-loving personality" correlated to "success in the work role." When stated this way, the problem with lack of correlation becomes obvious, but here the candidate's charming personality during the interview caused the hiring manager to decide he was a "good fit," when in reality, his charming personality made him a remarkably bad fit for both the job role and the company culture.

The path to a good hire begins with precision. You must decide what you are looking for in terms of actual behaviors. It's fine if you want to start with "fit"—ok, what does fit look like here? Do you really need a fun-loving personality in your systems architect? If you took the time to list out how you need your system architect to behave, "fun-loving" would likely not be anywhere near the top of your list. But most job descriptions don't even list behaviors. And the reason is because most people don't know where to begin. Importantly, the company in our example had a job description full of technical certifications and KSAs, but not a list of behaviors or behavioral characteristics—but then, they hired him because of the behavior he exhibited during the interview. Essentially, they hired him based on behaviors, even though they had no description of behaviors that correlate with success for that job.

Our starting point to solve this problem is to accept that behavior matters. How your employees actually behave at work, and more importantly, how they behave under stress, directly correlate with how they perform their work roles. And the only way to identify which behaviors correlate with success and which with failure is to establish a framework to determine why the good employee is good and why the poor performer is poor. When was the last time you took a minute to consider what it is about your best performer that makes her great? When was the last time you performed a review to determine the behaviors which lead to a termination? For most people, the top performer is a "rockstar"—which is meaningless. The low performer "just didn't work out"—also meaningless.

And that's why most people use defaults—because specifically identifying behavioral characteristics which correlate to success or failure is difficult. And that's what these "fit" labels are: generic defaults which seem as though they correlate to high job performance, but which actually do not. And that leads to the second problem, which is getting derailed by a false correlation. Being a "nice guy" is only relevant if being nice actually correlates to success in the job role for that company. The problem is the default presumption of "We're having a hard time finding somebody, so let's at least find a nice guy." And when you go in with that mindset, you're not going to come out with a nice guy. When you go in with a default mindset, you're going to come out with somebody who is a "good fit for the team," and that's somebody you're comfortable with—someone who is just like you.

Many organizations talk about their company culture and the idea of fitting into that culture. But on the flip side, it's vital to value differences in perspective, unique approaches to problem-solving, and diversity in general. This is especially true in the field of cybersecurity, because the stakes are so high. Without diverse mindsets and thought processes, you don't have a team; you have several people with one opinion. The reason high-functioning teams perform at a different level is because the process of working with different approaches produces a better result. Without differences of opinion and differences in thinking, your cybersecurity performance will suffer. When you start with the structure of, "What do I need?"—what are the technical things and what are the behaviors—the stuff that's not important will fall away. Mainly, "Do I feel one hundred percent comfortable with this person?" If you have finally found the unicorn that meets the things you need, nothing else will matter, because you're going to be so happy that you found the person that you need.

Teamwork can coexist with cultural differences. In fact, it can thrive with diversity. Yet, it's so difficult for people to hire someone when that person is someone different from themselves. The Big Mistake yet again. As Gail notes, we need different views to create better solutions:

> **Gail:** I tell people that I have a different perspective and the more perspectives you have, the better. I want to hear from everybody. I can't hear from enough people about what they think is important because everybody brings different experiences and insights to the table, and enhances the conversation. And the more of those people you can bring into the tent, the better your chance of avoiding a catastrophe. But sometimes that can be a struggle.[1]

Think back to the Equifax horror story and the conflicting personalities at the heart of it: a working relationship between the CIO and

---

[1] G. Gottehrer, in discussion with the authors. July 09, 2020.

his subordinate CSO devolving because of "fundamental disagreements," causing the removal of the security function from IT (out of the CIO's territory) into legal. Even when a new CIO was hired, and then a new CSO, this siloed structure never reverted.[2] While "fundamental disagreements" are unworkable, disagreements in general are not. Cybersecurity requires differing perspectives because every problem requires as close to 360-degree perspective as possible. Adam Bricker explains:

> **Adam:** We need the intellectual curiosity, and the emotional courage, to try to figure out the other side of the story—spending as much time proving ourselves right as proving ourselves wrong.[3]

There are some who would dispute placing capability first. This argument holds for the notion that "good people" should be found first and then projects found for them. It's a compelling argument. And in some ways, we agree with it. But while that works for strategic development and innovation, hiring for cybersecurity roles is more focused, so it requires a different approach. The "good people" process would be equivalent to assembling a group of good athletes and then finding a sport for them to play. That may work if you have the time and resources to find a group of athletes who are willing to accept employment without knowing what sport they'll play. But if you're building a soccer team, you'll have better success if you look for good soccer players. And while you may find some good athletes along the way whom you can teach soccer, it takes time and resources to teach them—just like you may find a talented leader who knows nothing about cybersecurity—you can teach them the tech side of cybersecurity, but it takes time and resources to do so. And you will probably find enough good soccer players that it makes no sense to spend time and resources teaching the game to good athletes who don't already know the rules.

---

[2] U.S. House of Representatives Committee on Oversight and Government Reform, *The Equifax Data Breach*. 115th Congress. https://republicans-oversight.house.gov/wp-content/uploads/2018/12/Equifax-Report.pdf (pp. 55–56).

[3] A. Bricker, in discussion with the authors. July 13, 2020.

It's the same for cybersecurity hiring. You need specific people who can do the work, but at some level, there are many people with the technical skill to do the job you're hiring for. So what's next?

Understanding Human Behavior

Companies must understand that what they're hiring is a set of behaviors. Just as there are no universal job descriptions, there are no universal optimal behaviors. Even when you decide to look at soccer players and not any other sport, you find everyone knows the game, but not everyone has the same level of skill and not everyone can play every position.

If you have memories of intramural sports during high school, or if you ever coached your kid's soccer team, it's a great way to illustrate the point. It was usually pretty easy to tell who the good soccer players were—they were always kicking around a soccer ball anyway. But they were generally the ones who could kick the ball where they wanted it to go—as opposed to the rest of us for whom it was a luck proposition at best. But regardless of their basic skill, everyone also knew what position the good players should play. There was always a high skill player who was a waste of talent on defense because she'd never stay there. As soon as she got the ball, she'd be off like a rocket and trying to score. As annoying as that would be, you quickly learned that her position should be striker. You'd probably win if she was there, and she was going to play there anyway. Similarly, there were others who had equal ball-handling talent who would simply never move forward. Regardless of the opportunity, as soon as they reached mid-field they would pass forward and hustle back to the penalty zone and set up for defense.

Put simply: you needed both types of players if you were going to win the soccer game at recess. And you need to match the personality (as distinct from the skill) to the position. In addition, the behaviors are not things which can be trained in or trained out. Ball-handling skill can be taught and developed through drills and practice. But the deep desire to protect the goal or the red-hot desire to score can't be taught. It can be identified during practice and utilized during the game, but it can't be created where it doesn't exist.

How does this apply to hiring for your cybersecurity team? First, and most important, you must identify the behaviors you need (as distinct from the skill). After the heavy lifting of *Can* and *Trust*, what you want is a hire who *Will* behave in the way you want them to behave—or, more accurately, how they need to behave to get the job done well. The only way to find such a candidate is to carefully parse how you need the person in the specific job role you are hiring for to behave. There may be major differences between what someone is capable of versus what he or she will accomplish. Why is this important? Because it's the performance of the team that matters. And here, we transition from soccer to watches.

We have a colleague who loves watches and has a collection, but the one we notice the most is a Rolex dive watch. We don't know enough to give the watch model name, but we've listened to our colleague speak about it enough to have a sense of what goes into its parts and assembly. Naturally, only the best materials are used, the correct alloys and jewels are procured, and the tiny parts are manufactured. The design is also nearly perfect and is the result of years of seeing how watches can be damaged, abused, or just subjected to routine wear and tear. But it's the assembly which is truly remarkable. When one of their expert assemblers puts the pieces together, a huge amount of time and attention is devoted to ensuring the pieces fit. What they don't do is grab parts from a box, snap them together, and screw on a casing. They painstakingly inspect each part to ensure it has been manufactured correctly and to standards. Then, they insert it where it belongs in the watch movement and test it to ensure it functions properly before the next piece goes in. If a part does not function properly, the assembler has a set of tools which can file, shape, and refine the part until it functions the way it should. If a part cannot be modified so it will work, it is discarded.

The process is painstaking and deliberate, but results in a set of parts coming together with a close enough fit that the watch functions perfectly. And not just perfectly—it functions perfectly under stress. Our colleague's watch can be dropped, banged against furniture, scratched across steel, and even taken down to one hundred meters under water, and it still functions perfectly. Why? Because the parts were manufactured of high-quality materials and—most importantly—fitted together with a high level of skill and attention to detail, so all of the parts function as one device even under stress.

This is why understanding behavioral characteristics is so important when hiring for your cybersecurity team. If you take care to ensure all the positions are filled with people who have the characteristics needed to fill each role, and your team is fitted together with care and precision, they will do the job of protecting your company, even under stress. And the fit is very specific. Let's go back to our funny, lively, high-spirited failure at the beginning of the chapter. For the company that hired him, that set of behavioral characteristics was disruptive and caused problems in how the team functioned. But in another company, one which needs an active cheerleader who bounces from cubicle to cubicle giving everyone approval and a quick break from the pressures of work, he would be a good member of the team. The point is simple and critically important: the team matters, each position on the team matters, and the behavior of each team member matters. Bill Thornton explains:

> **Bill:** On the issue of teamwork—every team can tolerate one or two eclectic people that can't get along and can't communicate but are so great, technically, that you're willing to overlook the problem. But it's very rare that the person is actually worthwhile. So it's communication and the ability to work in the group. You don't have to work perfectly or flawlessly, and collaborate on everything just right, but you've got to be able to communicate and effectively work together. Delegate, trust, responsibility, share it. Cooperate, collaborate, if you can't do any of those skills it's very difficult to have an effective team. And here's what I mean, I can put someone—unless you're again just staring at logs at the very entry level—if I put you in charge of my data loss protection program, you have to cooperate, you have to collaborate with business, with engineers, with everyone across the spectrum. If you can't do that—I have someone like that—I had to let them go. It's not fun but it's critical. It's a critical skill. I'm not saying

it's a panacea to cover up for inadequate technical skills, but if you don't have that skill, I'm really not very interested.[4]

All of the personalities must fit together to form one durable and high functioning whole. And parts are not interchangeable. A replacement gear from one Rolex will not simply pop into another Rolex—it needs to be fitted, modified, if necessary and possible, and tested. The fact that the candidate you are considering was successful with your competitor, or even with the company that you just acquired, does not mean they'll be successful with you. You simply must understand who and what they are: what they can do and what they will do—determine if they have the behavioral characteristics that correlate to success in the specific work role for your company.

Identifying Behavioral Characteristics

The best indication of behavior is past behavior—which is the portion that the final phase of our hiring model deals with: the Will.

Most hiring managers know whether a person will succeed within the first few months after hiring, usually during the onboarding period. Why is this significant? Because it means everyone knows what failure and success looks like within a few months of hiring. The problem is most hiring managers don't know soon enough—they know after hiring, but not before. How do you make better hiring decisions? Know before you make a job offer. The solution begins with one of the other core drivers of bad hiring decisions. We've already looked at what happens when you try to hire for "fit": you don't get a team, you get multiple people with one world view.

The other core driver of bad hiring decisions is Category-Based Presumptions. Things like, "Older people are reliable," or "Millennials are selfish." Fundamentally, these presumptions may be correct, but they simply aren't useful when you're hiring. Why? Because you're not hiring a class of people, you're hiring a person. Millennials might be selfish, but the actual young person sitting in your interview may not be. Older

---

[4] B. Thornton, in discussion with the authors. July 29, 2020.

people might be reliable, but the one sitting across from you might be a flake. How do you tell?

This problem is avoided by ensuring you know the specific behaviors required to be successful both with your company and in the specific job you are hiring for. The fundamental key to using behavioral characteristics to differentiate between candidates is to understand behaviors are specific to the job and to the individual, and the purpose of the hiring process is to connect them. Behavioral characteristics are not general—there is no generic set of behaviors which correlates generally with success or failure. While it's true that there are a variety of publicly available behavior profiles available without much searching, be aware using them can lead to bad hiring decisions, and in some cases, litigation.

The properly prepared and executed behavioral interview is crucial to getting this right. And it starts with asking: Who do you truly need? Begin by working through the particular job role and categorizing the behaviors of previous employees. (Remember, even if it's a "new job" for your company, someone may already be doing—or outsourcing—the work. That's probably why you're hiring, and it means you have behaviors to analyze.) As you work through this analysis, break down past behaviors into those which lead to success in the role and those which lead to failure.

Another issue to address here is the difference between what a person *Can* do and what they *Will* do. You may have a person who demonstrates a high level of skill in communication, someone who can fluently speak "tech" and "people," but if they don't speak "people" to those who need it because they don't want to, that's a performance difficulty which is extraordinarily difficult to correct. The tech person who isn't interested in communication unless you speak their language is really no different than the tech person who can't communicate at all. Both are probably Failure–Noncoachable. In fact, one of the critical components listed in the NICE Framework is the ability to communicate technical information in lay terms when necessary.[5] A candidate who can do this in a test environment may not be able to do it in an emergency. Worse, a candi-

---

[5] NICE Cybersecurity Workforce Framework. https://nvlpubs.nist.gov/nistpubs/SpecialPublications/NIST.SP.800-181.pdf (pp. 25–88).

date may have the capability of speaking in lay terms, but be unwilling to do so due to arrogance or other personality traits. The behavioral interview extracts this type of data and is a crucial part of the overall candidate evaluation when taken together with credentials and testing.

Once you have relevant behaviors delineated into Success, Failure–Coachable, and Failure–Noncoachable, add to this the list of hard skills, certifications, and training required to perform the role. These four lists (behaviors, hard skills, certifications, and training) are now the foundation for drafting the job description competencies—your articulation of who you are looking for.

Spotlight: Personality

It is important to distinguish between personality and behaviors, which are two different psychological concepts. Personality traits can influence our behavior in many cases, and there are hundreds of academic (and not-so-academic) studies and books written on this topic. But for our purposes, as discussed earlier, one of the key errors that leads to The Big Mistake is thinking that what you see of someone's "personality" during an interview reveals whether he or she is a "good fit." While you might think that the abundance of personality inventories available, and the broad range of differing approaches to psychological testing, personality typing, and personal potential indicator assessments, would provide something useful, these tests usually assess general traits like competence, work ethic, or emotional intelligence. An introspective review of these general personality traits may be helpful to an individual who is seeking self-development through reflection, but such testing is not helpful in determining whether a person is both capable and willing to execute a given cybersecurity job role for a particular employer.

We are not psychologists and do not claim to be. Our main point is this: the impact of failing to specifically identify the behavior characteristics—not general personality traits, but the specific behavior characteristics—which correlate with success and failure in a specific cybersecurity job role at a specific company—is exponentially greater than with a nontechnical position. Getting it wrong in the warehouse wreaks havoc in shipping; getting it wrong in network penetration puts the entire enterprise immediately at risk. Again, we are not dismissing introspection or these more generic personality traits as being without value; we are strong advocates for using them in self-development training programs. They are simply too general to correlate specifically enough to be relevant or useful in a hiring process.

Behaviors that correlate with success or failure in cybersecurity job roles must be precise enough to be useful. Bill Brennan highlights how he views certain behaviors fitting into cybersecurity job roles:

> **Bill**: If you're super detailed and you love following procedure, and that's where you're comfortable, in developing new procedures—my goodness, information security has a job for you. You can come be a risk analyst for me tomorrow, I would love it. But if you're a by-the-book-procedural person, you're not going to be a very good analyst. And vice versa, if you're kind of freeform, "I'm going to go where the bits take me but I'm going to get to a conclusion," my goodness, please join my analyst team but man I don't want you doing checklists because you're going to be unhappy.[6]

Personality traits are general descriptors that do not correlate to job performance; behavioral characteristics are specific descriptors that can correlate to job performance. Consequently, personality traits don't matter when attempting to find the right hire; behaviors do matter. If your personality assessment tests for emotional intelligence, it will not produce the differential data necessary to slot the detail-oriented procedure person into the information security job and the "follow the bits where they take me" person into the analytic group.

In order to truly visualize this concept in the context of cybersecurity job roles, let's take a look at exemplary behaviors that cybersecurity

---

[6] B. Brennan, in discussion with the authors. August 04, 2020.

professionals have called out. Amanda Tilley, the information security analyst, explains the confluence of traits that create "teachability":

> **Amanda:** I've learned over the years that teachability is an incredibly important trait. It's essential to have the drive and the resources to go find the answer on your own, but it's crucial to put ego aside and acknowledge one's limit. Utilizing your teammates' experiences and perspectives in a collaborative environment to reach a conclusion makes the entire team better. What makes our team successful is that we are all there for one another, no one on the team should feel like he or she is on an island.[7]

Let's break down what Amanda is actually doing here, because it's more than just stating that teachability is a success indicator for the work roles in her company. She's intuitively doing the deeper dive into what specific behavior characteristics are the component parts of teachability. They are as follows:

1. The willingness to say "I don't know."
2. Responding to not knowing with a visceral need to find the answer.
3. The willingness to freely admit not knowing the answer and seek help.

If she didn't do the deeper dive, she would be stuck looking for "teachability" in her interview. As a result, she would struggle during the interview to understand how "teachability" manifests itself in behaviors and would very likely end up with a fuzzy sense of whether a candidate "seems teachable." But by taking the time to get to this granular level, and to specifically articulate the three behavioral characteristics which are the components of teachability for this job role in her company, she has a structure upon which to build her interview question sets. And she avoids The Big Mistake because she knows exactly what to interview for. By

---

[7] A. Tilley, in discussion with the authors. July 02, 2020.

setting up behavioral question sets for the three component behaviors of teachability, she will extract differential data which will allow her to analyze whether a candidate is teachable and should be offered a job.

Michael Woodson, the Director of Information Security and Privacy, points out the significance of communication among his team members:

> **Michael:** You've got to be able to talk and communicate. You should be able to sit in a meeting, and I expect you to not talk techie. And for those that can't, and I have those in my camp, they go to a meeting with me or maybe somebody else that can. I never send just one person to a meeting, I always partner them up so they can have somebody to back them. I've had to teach them to "talk people." And what does that mean? You've got to be able to take it to the upper level.[8]

This description of communication is actually a very specific success indicator, and it can be taken in contrast to Amanda's example which has constituent components. Michael's example is specific enough that it does not need to be broken down further. The signal that a deeper dive should be considered comes from addressing the question: "What does that success indicator mean?" If the meaning is one thing (i.e., "Communication means 'talking people' when necessary"), then a deeper dive will probably not reveal more specific behavioral characteristics and you can start building corresponding behavioral question sets. In contrast, Amanda's teachability success indicator means three things, so a deeper dive to ensure that all of the components of teachability are articulated is worthwhile before beginning to build question sets.

Gail Gottehrer, the emerging technologies lawyer, describes a seemingly contradictory set of traits:

> **Gail:** This may seem contradictory, but I think the skill that is important is being flexible enough to be both proactive and reactive. You need somebody who can make a plan, can see a situation, assess risk and evaluate scenarios, and then look forward and come up with a plan to address the concerns that exist at the time and

---

[8] M. Woodson, in discussion with the authors. July 20, 2020.

those that are foreseeable and help keep the organization safe. But, the person also needs to be prepared to scrap that plan at pretty much a moment's notice and then come up with a new one, and not get hung up on the pride of ownership, or get defensive about perceptions that the original plan was "wrong," because, in the world of cybersecurity, the world changes in the blink of an eye.[9]

Gail articulates an excellent example of the complexity we see in the cybersecurity world, and it underscores why a deep level of precision is crucial when evaluating people for hiring in cybersecurity. Without a structure like Can–Trust–Will, which enables you to unpack and organize the technical skill and behavioral characteristics that correlate with success in specific job roles, you would—like many people do today—throw up your hands in frustration and say "just hire some good people!" But with a structure like Can–Trust–Will, Gail can articulate that she needs someone who can both create a plan and scrap the plan and improvise immediately upon seeing the plan won't work. And by deep diving into the component behaviors of planning and the component behaviors of scrapping-the-plan, she will be able to build focused question sets which will extract differential data for all of the behavioral characteristics she needs in the job role. It may be difficult to find people with all of the characteristics she needs, but—and this is most crucial—she knows what she's looking for. Consequently, if she doesn't find the candidates she needs and has to scrap her own plan, she'll be doing so with data that prove such candidates aren't available. And that allows her to either proceed with "Failure–Coachable" candidates who will be trained, or restructure the work roles within her team so employees with the two behavior characteristics are set up to interact in a way which produces success for the company.

Adam Lee, the VP and CSO, discusses his view of "flexibility" in our complex cybersecurity world:

Adam: It takes constant evolution. The threats evolve as fast or faster than your defenses. So every aspect from funding, to staffing, to what defenses are in place, to why you are doing what you

---

[9] G. Gottehrer, in discussion with the authors. July 09, 2020.

are doing, is a constantly evolving puzzle. You cannot have staff that are inflexible … you cannot have a vision that is stagnant or that is fighting the last war … you have to be nimble and evolving while still doing everything you did before, just as well as you did it before because threats don't go away. They get added to.[10]

How do you find the people you need to address threats which "evolve as fast or faster than your defenses?" Without a structure which drives a granular analysis to separately identify the technical skills and behavioral characteristics that correlate to success for each work role, you will simply fail to find and hire the people you need to stay ahead of the threat. Dive into the analysis to pull out each behavior that corresponds with success.

Uncommon Characteristics

We'll conclude this chapter with a few observations related to behavioral characteristics which many of us wish were common, but simply are not. This section is not a lament, nor is it advice that these behaviors should be more broadly sought or developed. Rather, we enumerate them to trigger your thought processes as you begin to understand what skills and behaviors correlate with success in your company. These things are uncommon and should be recognized, both so they don't find their way into every job description (you'll have to scrap that plan) and so you'll recognize them when you see them.

Adam Bricker offers a wonderful view on one of the more uncommon behaviors, "grit":

Adam: I've talked about curiosity, communication, storytelling, critical thinking, discipline, etc. Now we must add another dimension to the skill set—grit. I define grit as "doing the unpleasant when it's necessary, over and over again." And these professionals with grit—they're called at two or three o'clock in the morning, they're called on Saturday afternoons, they're called on Monday. And it's really unpleasant sometimes—what they deal with, the

---

[10] A. Lee, in discussion with the authors. July 09, 2020.

false positives, the false negatives, the nation-state actors and persistent threats, and whatever else there might be out there. But over and over again, they have demonstrated that ability to consistently answer the call.[11]

This characteristic is complex, rare, and extraordinary. The person who won't quit when they find themselves in difficulty is unusual but not particularly rare. It's not perseverance in the face of adversity which makes grit rare, but it's the willingness to enter a situation which is known to be difficult, to choose to face the same challenge again, which makes grit rare. In addition, grit is also so deep-rooted in the people who have it, that most of them don't even realize they have grit—they think they're just doing what needs to be done. Consequently, grit is not only rare but also often unacknowledged and difficult to detect. It's worthwhile to be aware of the concept and existence of grit, and to ensure you have it in the description for the few job roles which require it.

Curiosity is often mentioned alongside passion in the world of cybersecurity. They are not the same, but their interlocking nature underscores the significance of such characteristics in certain cyber roles. For John Avenson,[12] the Vice President of Technology for the Major League Baseball Team the Minnesota Twins, curiosity is so important that he calls it a superpower:

John: If human beings have any superpower, it's curiosity. While we try to hire technology folks that meet our educational and skills focused job description requirements, we tend to put more emphasis on the traits and aptitudes a candidate can holistically offer. Does their curiosity drive a passion that looks for opportunity? Does their curiosity fuel a spirit to discover and innovate within a small team? We need to hire folks that leverage their

---

[11] A. Bricker, in discussion with the authors. July 13, 2020.

[12] John Avenson began his twenty-seventh season with the Minnesota Twins baseball team in 2020, and he was named Vice President of Technology in 2006. John is a veteran of the Persian Gulf War, where he served with the United States Marine Corps.

curiosity to want to wear multiple technology hats while keeping their head on a business swivel. These kinds of hires are especially important for small or medium sized businesses who don't have a specialized team working in an independent Cybersecurity Operations Center.[13]

The way John articulates curiosity reveals it as a way of being, rather than merely a behavioral characteristic—and at his sophisticated level, it is. It's reminiscent of Adam's "essential life skills" from Chapter 3, the deep component of who and what a person is which makes them "unable to not" figure things out. Our best advice regarding the superpower of curiosity is to ensure you are always on the lookout for it during your behavioral interview and snatch it up when it suits your open role.

Speaking further to passion, it is a complex behavior which is commonly referenced in cybersecurity—whether it is being defined as desire to grow, to learn, or to advance. Wheeler Coleman gives us his take:

Wheeler: I love taking a strong number two employee and making that person the number one (a lead role such as a CISO). So, whether it's at a conference, through LinkedIn or other social media, I'm looking for hungry, talented people. They want to prove themselves and are looking for an opportunity to set the world on fire. I once recruited a guy that was a strong number two itching to get a title of CISO. He had a boss that was doing well and not leaving his position anytime soon. He jumped at the opportunity to make a difference.[14]

There are two forces at work in Wheeler's description. In some ways, it's a mentor–protégé interaction, but at its core, it's a person with a very specific set of drivers having the path cleared by someone who knows the way and values unlocking the potential seen in someone else. The behavioral characteristic of having a "hunger" is what identifies a person with development potential. But without a corresponding behavioral

---

[13] J. Avenson, in discussion with the authors. August 03, 2020.

[14] W. Coleman, in discussion with the authors. August 12, 2020.

characteristic in Wheeler's personality—that of coach, mentor, instructor, and developer—the potential of the employee would either remain untapped or would require a struggle to emerge. We won't do a deep dive into leadership here, but the observation is that while identifying behavioral characteristics is key to finding the people you should hire, it's fostering the interactions between the people on your team that drives high performance. As difficult as it is to find and hire people, the effort is wasted unless leaders take action to unlock the potential they bring.

Spotlight: Legacy Systems

Many of the cybersecurity leaders we interviewed spoke about the challenge of joining mature organizations that already had existing teams but needed to go through the process of cultural change to grow to the next level. The challenge when taking over a team, regardless of size, is how to create a process to make the necessary change without causing undue disruption. These CIOs, CISOs, and IT leads had to handle a different type of "legacy" system, and it is a complex situation to manage.

It's easy for the new boss to come in, "clean house" (i.e., fire key people), and bring in their own team—a bunch of new key people. But often, the shock of the change causes more problems than it solves. There's a better way, and it relies on understanding of the behavioral characteristics which correlate to success in each job role in order to influence the change needed. It's like the difference between liposuction and a program of diet and exercise when you need to lose weight. Liposuction is drastic and has an immediate and apparent effect, but it may not produce durable results. Diet and exercise do not show immediate results, but when change comes, it is both durable and inexorable. And although the change can happen gradually enough that you might wonder if it will happen at all, it will happen with purpose.

When you take a new job, particularly if it is a senior role, most of the advice you'll get is about taking the time to learn your environment and understand your people. And it's important to take that time to understand the behavioral characteristics of the people you have and begin figuring out the behavioral characteristics you need as you restructure the team. But it's equally important to recognize that the process of taking some time also allows your environment to become familiar with you being in it. If you come in and start pushing, everyone is still trying to understand who you are and how you communicate. If you immediately put them under the stress of change, of doing the old things in a different way, performance suffers. And it suffers for a very specific reason. You've come into their environment which is familiar to them, and you want them to be different.

Many leaders talk about listening tours, and how important it is to not do anything for the first six weeks or even for the first six months before truly understanding the environment. Fundamentally, the listening tour is not actually about them understanding the environment—it's them recognizing the environment takes time to understand and get familiar with them. In the same way you start losing weight by doing small things every day that cause the fat cells to leave the body, so to, you're interacting with people in a way that draws to you the personalities, and the behavior types that function best with you. This process will also drive away the behaviors and personality types that don't function well—whether that's personnel leaving on their own, or being let go as the process moves forward. And if you focus on understanding the behavioral characteristics you have and then determine the ones you need, the change will become a process of managing how the personalities interact and how the team culture changes as people depart and replacements arrive.

CHAPTER 5

Hiring the Right Cybersecurity Role Behaviors

Now for the next pieces in the puzzle: determining what behaviors lead to success in what cybersecurity roles and setting up corresponding behavioral interviews. The purpose of the behavioral interview question sets is to cause the candidate to think, to dig, and to reveal behavioral characteristics which will predict actual future behavior in the workplace. Behavioral questions call for the sharing of an experience which reveals or illustrates a behavioral characteristic relevant to the job, and upon which the hiring manager can differentiate candidates. In short, behavioral interviews should uncover behavioral characteristics, not just instances of past action. And to design question sets which reveal the relevant behavioral characteristics, you must first specifically identify what those behavioral characteristics are for each job.

Role Descriptors … in a Perfect World

Cybersecurity roles change every minute of every day. Inherent responsibilities, expectations, and knowledge needs vary based on industry. Marie explains her approach to work:

> **Marie:** I don't have a traditional background in cybersecurity and technology—I'm just a naturally curious person. When interviewing, they knew I had potential. I'm a quick and independent learner. Working in tech and IT gave me more of an opportunity to figure out how to poke around at things and understand how to break and fix them. There were times when I'd have a stack of

computers to my right side that I'd have to run through re-imaging them or swapping out parts, while I was working on various software activities, and still helping out end users learn how to use the printers or whatever they needed assistance with in that moment.[1]

The behaviors Marie is inherently referring to are curiosity, desire to learn, and the ability to multitask. As a cybersecurity project manager, it makes sense that she is successful! In combination with the requisite technical skills, Marie has something more than a strong drive to learn, it's more of a drive to figure things out. The actual behavioral characteristic is the combination of a nearly compulsive drive to solve puzzles, a contentment when enveloped with things to do, and the need to continually explore. Her comment about understanding "how to break and fix" things is particularly revealing: a broken thing is not "bad," so there is no stress or pressure to get it fixed to stay out of trouble. To her, something broken is an opportunity to explore, tinker, and fix. The creative destruction process matters to her.

The role descriptors we offer later in this chapter are illustrative and intended to inspire. While noting, importantly, that cybersecurity positions must always be specifically defined by the employer for each job role, what we provide below is a general framework within which job role functions can be matched with correlating behavioral characteristics. Adam Lee explains how his organization attempts to balance technical skills (*Can*) and behaviors (*Will*), alongside diversity and career lifecycle goals:

> **Adam:** I mean we're balancing a lot of company goals in our hiring practices: we have diversity goals, we have career lifecycle goals for the folks that are on board, we have a whole lot of things that interrupt the direct recruitment-hiring pipeline. There are other factors that we have to consider as we hire folks. I'm finding that in the cybersecurity area, we need a balance of squared-away folks that are smart in analytic discipline, but they're also very technical,

---

[1] M. Chudolij, in discussion with the authors. July 24, 2020.

and that's the hardest thing. Because if you're just a network architect or you're just kind of an IT type, just kind of a core-geek type,
IT person, it's sort of a different skill set than having the patience
and focus of somebody building use cases for your SIEM, and
sitting there and working cases in terms of when they're seeing.
Some folks aren't cut out for it but it's a difficult balance because
you also need that technical skill set.[2]

For perspective, let's frame this back into our *Can–Trust–Will* model.
To grasp the challenge Adam articulates here, the approach is crucial, otherwise you risk getting overwhelmed. It's the structure of *Can–Trust–Will*
which keeps you on track. As Adam describes, it's easy to get distracted
when reviewing candidates who are highly qualified in the technical
arena, but appear to be a poor match for the communications and teamwork requirements. The key is to understand that the tech requirements
are both easy to find and easy to filter for—they are binary: can the candidate do the tech work, or can't they? That's *Can*, and it's quick, easy, and
high volume. It's also inevitable that most of the tech-qualified (and tech-
trainable) candidates, those that *Can*, are also not going to be hired. But
that's because the behavioral characteristics are more rare and more difficult to find. As Bill Thornton explains:

> **Bill:** There are people that have lots of certifications and still can't
> find their way out of a paper bag. And so, the interviews have to
> be a lot more probing to understand the technical skills. And then
> there's a level of interpersonal skill with some of our people, par-
> ticularly in this industry; there are people that just don't have the
> requisite people skills for managers. And so we have a dichotomy
> sometimes between business people managing technical people,
> which is fine if they're immersed in the technology, otherwise
> it creates a schism that—because the two can't communicate—
> I think places the company at increased risk.[3]

---

[2] A. Lee, in discussion with the authors. July 09, 2020.
[3] B. Thornton, in discussion with the authors. July 29, 2020.

Consequently, it's crucial to structure your process of filters so each succeeding pool is more refined. Once you have the *Can* pool established, and you've gone through the *Trust* phase, the most difficult piece of our model awaits—the behavioral interview, which extracts *Will*. You'll then have the candidates to whom you should extend offers. Many employers, recruiters, and hiring managers refer to behaviors as "soft skills" or "the non-techie stuff." If the conversation calls for this type of language, we consider the category of behavior important enough to call them "foundational skills." But regardless of how you've understood them before or what you call them, the most important aspect is to appreciate the value of behaviors as part of a job description, particularly with regard to how they correlated with job success. Paul Casale, using the term "soft skills," highlights this "narrowing" process:

> **Paul:** Where our sales team comes in, which is invaluable to us, is talking directly to managers, building relationships and really narrowing down not only what the responsibilities and main skills are, but what they really want to see in someone. They find what type of skill background they want them to come from, what kind of company or industry they want them to come from, the soft skills that may not always be in the job description. We then may even target companies that the manager may find would help a new hire adapt professionally and culturally.[4]

Obviously, in a perfect world, employers would get to choose from a talent pool bursting with "positive" characteristics including ability to multitask, ability to communicate, ability to remain calm under fire, and ability to exhibit a proactive mentality.

But not all roles need these ideal traits; some positions are actually well-served by behaviors that have negative connotations. What if your open role actually needs a candidate who is selfish, self-entitled, impatient, or overly critical? A great general example of this is the successful delivery driver. Anyone successful in this role needs to be a bit selfish;

---

4 P. Casale, in discussion with the authors. June 26, 2020.

otherwise they'll spend too much time looking for legal parking instead of double parking, making the delivery, and quickly getting on to the next customer. And that includes men and women, all ages and all colors. But the very best of them roll right down Main Street, block traffic, go to three different locations on foot, and then go on their way. It's not that they don't care—but it just doesn't register. Why? Because they're prickly, and all they care about is knocking out their deliveries and getting onto the next one. Recognizing the value in that prickly attitude is extremely important. It's a behavioral characteristic which correlates to success in the job role.

In cybersecurity, there are many roles that may require seemingly negative behaviors. For example, however you label the job that is tasked with handling internal employees who have mistakenly clicked on a phishing e-mail: that employee must be able to act in a disciplinary function frequently. You to be able to effectively say, "Listen you really screwed this up, and it's really important that you not do this again," and have them respond, "You know what, you're right. And I know that you're the tech nerd who lives in the basement, but I really appreciate you coming up here and sharing the importance of this problem with me." You have to have a certain amount of drive, a certain aggressive nature to you, tempered with restraint and diplomacy. And you have to be unconcerned if the person you are speaking with is a mid-level accountant or the Chairman of the Board. This role could also likely include the requirement to tell senior employees—from the best sales person, to the managing partner, to the CIO—that they simply must participate in the new dual-factor authentication program (and, unfortunately, it typically is the more senior employees that refuse). To be able to say, "Listen, I know you're in charge," but still—"We have to have a talk," while remaining forceful and respectful. You are telling them something that you know they don't want to hear, but you are going into that conversation saying, "Look, I know you bring a lot of money into this firm but as much as you're bringing money into this company, I am making sure that money doesn't leak out the bottom of the ship." It takes a unique personality to come in and say, "This is important. I get that you don't think that this is important, but it really is—and here's why." And that you won't let it go any more than the managing partner or CIO is going to let anything go that they think is important, because you are both a part of the team.

Spotlight: the New Perspective

An IT team lead for a software company came in needing advice on interviewing. The company was hiring twenty new people for its call center and five team leads (one of whom was our client) had been gathered together by their executive, handed a stack of applicant files, and told to "hire the best ones" (sound familiar?). Without any training or experience with interviewing or candidate evaluation, the team leads were struggling to select candidates who would succeed, or even just make it past ninety days. During our initial consultation we also learned that the company was struggling with a turnover rate of over sixty percent. Our client indicated that the candidates he hired seemed great during the interview and then either struggled to do the work or quickly engaged in disruptive behavior. Some quit, others had to be fired.

We quickly learned the team leads were interviewing candidates by doing what most people do: They would read the file and then sit across from an applicant and ask questions off their resumés. "I see you graduated from here, what was that like?" "I see you worked there, what was that like?" During our initial consultation, our client was very frustrated and he wanted to know how poor performers were slipping through their process. "How can they look so good in the interview and then be so bad when they show up for work?" We hear this question regularly, so we asked what has become our key initial question: "How long after hiring do you know whether a new person will succeed or fail?" His answer: "About two weeks." This is typical, and also the best possible answer for us, because it leads us directly into the process of identifying the behavioral characteristics which form the foundation for the behavioral interview. The second question is: "Ok, how do you know? What does failure look like? What does success look like?"

Over the course of the next twenty minutes, we listened while he described in rather frustrated detail exactly what he observed in a person which made them fail and, on the rare occasions when they hired someone good, what made them succeed. After a few follow-up questions, we presented him a bullet point list of the four most important behavioral characteristics which he had identified as correlating with either success or failure in the job role. He confirmed the list, and within a week, we had question sets back to him for his next set of interviews.

Two months later we got a call and listened to his fascinating story. The interviews were done in groups—with the five team leaders interviewing approximately seven to ten candidates in a group (no kidding!). Four of the leads continued with their off-the-resumé questions. But when it was our client's turn to speak, he proceeded with our behavioral questions in the "Tell me about a time when …" format. He indicated that the entire attitude in the room immediately shifted: the applicants started paying attention and giving thoughtful answers. And the other team leads began taking notes on the answers now being provided. Upon evaluating the results of the interview, our client hired two candidates that the rest of his colleagues had summarily rejected. In fact (and now he was laughing on the phone), the other four team leads teased him and told him he was "crazy" for hiring "losers." His colleagues hired the same type of person they always selected. Six weeks later, both of the people he had hired based on his analysis of the behavioral interview were top performers, and every single one of his fellow team leads had at least one (and several had two) of their new hires either on performance improvement programs or termination trajectories, and a few of their new hires had already quit.

What was the difference? Our client changed his selection process based on what we taught him. And he did the most difficult thing which confronts someone who is just learning how to conduct behavioral interviews. He hired someone different. When you transition into a behavioral interview system, the first thing you'll notice is the analysis will have you hire people you would have passed on before. And it will have you pass on the people you would have hired before. Now, this makes intuitive sense when the process is viewed as an academic exercise. Your old system resulted in bad hires and a high turnover rate, so to be better, your new system should cause you to hire different people. But it's difficult because when you hire for fit and when you interview off the resumé, your process filters for "people like me" and the interview exists to confirm that feeling—and you're back to making The Big Mistake. It's confirmation bias at work. When you use a behavioral interview to extract differential data which correlate with success within the job role you are hiring for, very often that person will not "be like me," but they will be who you need.

So what's the challenge? The challenge is passing on the person who makes you feel comfortable and hiring the person who makes you feel uncomfortable. The good news? As you get more comfortable hiring people who make you feel uncomfortable, but who have the behavioral characteristics which correlate to job success, you'll find you have a diverse workforce that performs at the highest level. What our hero learned is, it's not whether he's happy to see this person—it's whether the new hire will get the job done. What he did was counterintuitive; he wasn't hiring the person he was most comfortable with—he was hiring the uncomfortable, based on an analysis of "this is the behavior that I need in this role." It takes a certain level of maturity to hire somebody that you might not want to invite to your house. In this case, maturity is revealed by understanding someone who is not like you, and through understanding them, getting to like them, in addition to valuing what their behavioral profile allows them to do.

And now we come to the general descriptors promised earlier in this chapter. The models offered in this book (which focus on cybersecurity and positions that inherently incorporate major cybersecurity aspects) should serve as a road map for certain types of roles and as a guide to the hiring process generally. Keep in mind as you review this section that every company interprets each of these roles a little differently, depending on corporate culture, industry needs, internal systems, and number of employees on the payroll. These are overviews which provide general categories of technical skills and behaviors that will get you started. But this is a departure point from which you must do your analysis to determine the behavioral characteristics which correlate with success for specific job roles at your company.

1. Chief Information Security Officer (executive level)
   - Technical skills:
     ◦ Create, develop, and keep current IT security policies, procedures, strategy, architecture alongside relevant C-Suiters.
     ◦ Consistently review and proactively improve information security programs and guidelines.

- ○ Implementation of necessary security standards (i.e., ISO, NIST, and SOC).
- ○ Implementation of security audits, tabletop exercises, and penetration testing.
- ○ Balance between security and innovation.
- • Behavior characteristics:
  - ○ Calm and focused under major stress.
  - ○ Organized multitasker.
  - ○ Communicates opinions with ease.
  - ○ Ability to clearly direct people.
  - ○ Solid decision-making skills.
  - ○ High confidence in ability to problem solve.

2. Network Engineer (mid- to senior level)
   - • Technical skills:
     - ○ Build, maintain, improve network.
     - ○ Handle network design upgrades.
     - ○ Investigate relevant new technologies.
     - ○ Monitor network performance.
     - ○ Troubleshooting and responding to help desk in conjunction with IT.
     - ○ Work with IT to plan, design, deploy new technologies and functions.
   - • Behavior characteristics:
     - ○ Quick reflexes.
     - ○ Passionate about subject area.
     - ○ Reviews information and situations critically.
     - ○ Note: Does not have to be major "team player" or very socially capable, but able to communicate across teams.
     - ○ Attention to detail.
     - ○ Problem-solver mentality.
     - ○ Time management.

3. Incident Responder (senior level)
   - • Technical skills:
     - ○ Evaluate and implement technical solutions, including artificial intelligence, big data analysis, and new technologies, to protect corporate information.

- o Integrate incident response with governance and compliance.
  - o Ensure current and consistent practices alongside legal, regulatory/compliance, and CISO.
  - o Monitor for events that could lead to an incident
- Behavior characteristics:
  - o Quick reflexes.
  - o Good communicator.
  - o Reviews information and situations critically.
  - o Can handle pressure well.
  - o Can act without emotion in stressful situations.
  - o Thorough.
  - o Attention to detail.
  - o Able to jump start.

4. Systems Administrator (entry level)
  - Technical skills:
    - o Support and system access control.
    - o Support maintenance and integration of authentication systems.
    - o Administer and support user administration.
    - o Assist in security program management.
    - o Research and report on current security threats.
    - o Assist with IT helpdesk.
  - Behavior characteristics:
    - o Social skills.
    - o Thorough researcher.
    - o Able to take direction with ease.
    - o Able to take criticism without emotional sensitivity.
    - o Good communicator.

Spotlight: Grace Under Fire

This wasn't just another crisis. All of the backups were infected—and the virus was spreading to the backups of the backups, which were unfortunately connected. This was a traditional mid-size law firm, where senior partners vehemently objected to new technologies, and the budget for the cybersecurity team was always a battle. The CISO was quickly briefed with a phone call at three in the morning, at which point she was raring to go. Her plan of action was pointed: get on site, brainstorm with her team, and call for backup as necessary. In this story, we were the vendor and were sincerely shocked by the level of calm with which the CISO presented the problem. She effectively and efficiently explained the situation and what steps had already been taken, without placing blame anywhere on the spectrum; she methodically talked through all options that we offered. We all came together to stop the virus in its tracks, and then moved forward with a plan to deal with the aftermath of the disaster.

This outcome would have been impossible with a CISO who had different behavioral characteristics. Even with the exact same team with the exact same technical skills, the outcome would have been dramatically different. What a person actually does in a crisis is driven by who they are. And who they are is the sum of their behavioral characteristics. And if you specify what behaviors the job role needs, you can find them.

Uncovering Behaviors

Technical skill matters. Experience matters. But as we've just read, action matters even more. This is where we move past the technical performance aspects of a good employee, the *Can*, and on to behaviors, the *Will*, which is the glue that holds everything together. Uncovering the employment-focused behavioral characteristics for your particular organization's cybersecurity jobs is essential to an effective hiring process. Adam Bricker highlights the balance between technical skills and behaviors:

> **Adam:** Technical skills are super important, but combined with effective communication, collaboration, and character, you now have the ability to consistently affect how someone else makes decisions, how somebody else gets focused on what is truly important (not just urgent).[5]

---

[5] A. Bricker, in discussion with the authors. July 13, 2020.

Behaviors that correlate with success in certain job roles allow for team success, and failure is expensive. According to the U.S. Department of Labor, a bad hiring decision can cost a company as much as thirty percent of the employee's annual salary—and the expense only goes up with seniority.[6] Employment-focused behavioral characteristics can act as the single best predictor of successful job performance. Bill Brennan hones in on how he uncovers behaviors that lead to success in certain cyber roles:

> **Bill:** If I'm a cyber defense analyst—I'm looking for people who are inquisitive. I'm looking for the people that are going to come into an interview and say "Hey, sorry I'm a little tired—I was doing this puzzle last night and I couldn't find this piece and I couldn't go to bed until I solved it." Well, cool, I can deal with a couple of hairs out of place—that's how you look at the world. If you're an Information Assurance person who's doing compliance audits, I want someone who is very detail focused. Show me things in your background or give me a way to draw out as I go through my interview process, even if it's not directly in your work experience, those things that I believe are transferable skills.[7]

In many ways, the technical skill, the *Can*, is the raw material. It's straight-grain pine to the homebuilder, curly maple to the cabinetmaker, high-carbon steel to the toolmaker, and fine silk to the dressmaker. But what is it that turns the maple into an heirloom table? What makes silk into a perfectly fitted blouse? It's the ability to see what the raw material can become if it's used properly. And in cybersecurity, the raw material of technical skill becomes the final product of security through tightly coordinated interaction. We call it *Will,* but to understand what a person will do, as opposed to what they can do, requires an understanding of willingness—the combination of capability and action. A person may be capable of producing a masterpiece, but if they don't sit in front of the easel

---

6 F. Fatemi. September 28, 2016. "The True Cost of a Bad Hire—It's More Than You Think." *Forbes.* www.forbes.com/sites/falonfatemi/2016/09/28/the-true-cost-of-a-bad-hire-its-more-than-you-think/#a72bc2f4aa41

7 B. Brennan, in discussion with the authors. August 04, 2020.

and put paint on canvas, no masterpiece will emerge. Fundamentally, and particularly in the security world, a person's brilliance is irrelevant unless it is coupled with action. Action which directly correlates to the outcome you need. *Can* is important, but what a person *Will* do is fundamental. And the best method to determine what a person *Will* do is a behavioral interview.

Behavioral interviews require more resources than the resumé-based interview. In addition to crafting the right behavioral question sets, hiring managers may need to be trained on best interview practices, and train other employees as well—time and expenses that come with implementing new procedures. So does every single candidate that reaches the *Will* phase need the behavioral interview? Yes. Absolutely.

The behavioral interview is a digging process, a deep dive into the history of behavior of each candidate who makes it to the *Will* phase. You are extracting differential data which correlate with success in the job role. But much of what you learn about each candidate will be Failure–Coachable, and some will be Failure–Noncoachable. Consequently, as you work through the question sets and help the candidate dig for relevant stories to share, you are also beginning to assess the data as the candidate shares it with you. And as you get better at conducting the behavioral interview, you will develop the ability to make accurate initial assessments regarding which data go in Failure–Coachable, which are Failure–Noncoachable, and which indicate Success. And just because a candidate has made it this far and has taken time out of a busy schedule to attend the interview does not render that candidate somehow more qualified. If a candidate is clearly Failure–Noncoachable through the first few questions, then doing anything other than ending the interview early and advising the candidate they will not be hired is unfair to the candidate and a waste of time for both of you. If you know what you're looking for because you have done the deep analytic work, you will continually be surprised at how very quickly you know whether any given candidate possesses or does not possess the behavior characteristics your job role requires.

This is one of the first lessons woodworkers learn. Many come into the hobby thinking that they will spend most of their time cutting and shaping wood. They quickly find that joinery depends on the precision of the cut, and the precision of the cut depends on how the tools are set up.

As a result, most of the time spent in woodworking is devoted to setting up tools and rechecking to ensure everything is correct before turning on the power. The cut itself only takes a few seconds. The behavioral interview is the same—it takes a good deal of time to set up correctly, but sometimes just a few minutes is all that is required to know whether you have the right person, or someone you can train to be what you need, or someone who will find success in some other job role at another company.

For large companies with vast cybersecurity teams, behavioral interviews for what Wheeler Coleman calls the "worker bees" might seem unnecessary, but as Wheeler points out, upward mobility and the changing nature of the field inherently support the importance of the behavioral interview for all:

> **Wheeler:** I believe that behavioral interviewing should be an integral part of all job interviews. For IT roles, we tend to focus on the technical matters such as whether candidates know their craft, and whether they understand the concepts and the technology around it. Typically, the "worker bees" are not necessarily hired based on their personality or their soft skills. For example, I've hired many technicians with great technical skills, but they had no personality. As a result, I couldn't put them in front of internal or external clients and customers. Instead, I would leverage their technical expertise and never expose them to clients. Even though the nature of technology allows specialists to only interact with their devices and the software, the tide is changing. And, of course, the higher up you are in the organization, soft skills are extremely important to be successful.[8]

For smaller companies, the behavioral interview is definitely a necessity. With smaller cybersecurity teams, everyone is put in the spotlight. As Austin Berglas explains, every team member on a smaller team wears multiple hats:

---

[8] W. Coleman, in discussion with the authors. August 12, 2020.

Austin: Everyone on my team is prepared. If you're on a call and a client says hey, we have a question about the threat hunt that you just did, then we all turn to the analyst, who has two years' work experience out of college, who is responsible for doing that threat hunt, he has to come up with the answers for the client. So, everybody needs to be client-facing, it's just, depending on the level of seniority, how much expectation is there for actually meeting a future client.[9]

Within a smaller cybersecurity team, everyone becomes client-facing; everyone knows each other; and the team dynamic is more pronounced. The behavioral interview is the only way to determine whether a candidate is willing to interact in the way the boss needs, the team needs, and the client needs.

We've spent a good deal of time discussing efficiency in the *Can–Trust–Will* process. And the efficiencies are important to extracting the data you need in a cost-effective way. Behavioral interviews are difficult and require the most time and resources of the three phases. So, while placing the behavioral interview at the end of your hiring process makes it a lower volume and less time-consuming step than it would otherwise be, it will still be where you spend most of your time and resources. *Can* and *Trust* are the steps which allow you to focus your binary decision making where it will have the most effect. These first two phases are where you find and refine your raw material. The hard work is the behavioral interview. But it's worth the effort.

Frequently, cybersecurity professionals do not have typical backgrounds—this is a truth clarified in earlier chapters. The behavioral interview allows the hiring manager to seek out the desired behaviors by digging into all experiences, not just cybersecurity-themed professional experience. As Bill Brennan explains:

Bill: I was hiring for a position nine months ago, and the guy had just finished his master's in cybersecurity, but didn't really have

---

[9] A. Berglas, in discussion with the authors. June 30, 2020.

any practical experience. But I ended up talking to him for twenty minutes on his experience as a professional musician. And he kind of stopped me eventually and said, "Listen, I really appreciate the interest and I'll talk music with you all day but I don't get it—why do you care?" I said, "Well, music composition, the ability to create, the ability to manage all the complexities of being the tour manager like you're talking about—those are all transferable skills to what I'm interviewing you for." And he said, "Oh, yeah, I guess you're right."[10]

Bill understands the difference between behavior and application. The behavior is the candidate's willingness to do what Bill needs done. The application, whether it's in music or network penetration, is much less relevant. John Avenson echoes this sentiment, with a different anecdote:

John: A few years ago, we were looking for a help desk person. Among the many applicants was a Marine veteran who was in transition back to civilian life. He was looking for a job in IT while working toward a degree in technology. We asked a typical question relating to handling stress—something like, "Give us a sense of how you handle pressure, perhaps when a server's not working or when the network is down." He admitted honestly that he could not answer the question because he did not yet have those IT experiences. Knowing he could handle stress, I rephrased the question—asking him to give an example of an experience in the Marine Corps where he worked through a stressful situation. He told a story of how he and a couple other Marines needed to fix a broken CH-46 helicopter that landed in the middle of the desert during active wartime in Iraq. They needed to get the helicopter in the air within a few hours, otherwise it would be demolished. Well, that mentality is what we look for: somebody who can take charge and solve a crisis without necessarily waiting for somebody else, or someone who can take on that risk and responsibility. He

---

[10] B. Brennan, in discussion with the authors. August 04, 2020.

got the job. His aptitude enabled rapid technology skill set growth, and he is now taking charge as Target Field's Broadcast Engineer.

Again, you need to know what you are looking for, with a well-thought-out job description. The right behaviors could come from musicians to Marines, as long as they are tech trainable.

Spotlight: Teamwork and Trust (and the Uber Data Breach)

A terrifying amount of data was stolen as part of the 2016 Uber data breach: 600,000 drivers' names and driver's license information, and the names, e-mail addresses, and phone numbers of fifty-seven million Uber riders.[11] But these staggering numbers aren't even the truly terrible part of this breach; what's worse is that Uber attempted to cover it up. The hackers apparently e-mailed Uber detailing their access and asking for money—and the (now former) Uber Chief Security Officer and his senior deputy took the bait, paying them $100,000 to keep the incident under the radar.[12]

How could this happen? And we don't mean the breach. Cybersecurity is a lot like riding a motorcycle. They say there are two kinds of riders: those that have gone down on the pavement, and those who will go down. In cybersecurity, the dichotomy is those who know they've been breached, and those who don't know they've been breached. Breaches happen, they are a nasty part of the cybersecurity world. But this is not about the breach. This is about the response, and how a person capable of such a terrible response could ever find their way into a position of such great responsibility.

Since everyone in cybersecurity knows the risks of breaches happening and also knows what to do in a data breach situation, how could a person, skilled enough in cybersecurity to be selected for the role of CSO

---

[11] Uber. *2016 Data Security Incident.* www.uber.com/newsroom/2016-data-incident/

[12] D. Etherington. *Uber Data Breach from 2016 Affected 57 Million Rider's & Drivers.* TechCrunch. https://techcrunch.com/2017/11/21/uber-data-breach-from-2016-affected-57-million-riders-and-drivers/

at a company the size of Uber, essentially run, hide, and lie when disaster struck? The answer starts with looking at the observed behavior and, in an almost detached way, asking: "How must a person feel in order to act that way? How must a CSO be feeling to run, hide, and attempt to cover up a data breach which most assuredly cannot be covered up?"

Panic? Sure, he panicked. But we need to go deeper—why the panic? In general, a panicked cover up happens when a person feels: "OMG— if people find this out, I'll lose my job." That's the visceral drive which causes a person to panic, then scramble, and often engage in a variety of self-destructive and sometimes criminal behaviors. But let's go deeper— what is the root cause of the "OMG, I'll lose my job" feeling? Part of the answer for any given person may be found in the corporate culture. If the company operates on a blame-and-terminate paradigm, then the fear of losing your job is rational. If someone gets fired every time something bad happens, then you can expect to be fired, and there's really nothing to be done about it. But let's look at the situation where that type of corporate culture does not exist. What happens in a corporate culture where blame is not assigned when disaster strikes? Do people in these "non-blame" cultures never fear being fired? Or is there something more? A person who fears being fired in a nonblame culture doesn't panic because of a rational fear of being fired; he panics because he doesn't have belief in himself.

What does that mean? The people who panic become focused on lying and covering up to save themselves and do so because they think they can't fix the problem. They have a deep-seated lack of faith in their own abilities. They don't think they can respond effectively; they don't think they can respond quickly enough; they don't think they can rely on the people around them; they don't think the team can solve the problem; and they don't think they can solve it either. Furthermore, they don't even think they can clean up the mess well enough to save themselves. They get overwhelmed and panic for one reason: lack of self-confidence; more specifically, a lack of confidence in their own ability to do what needs to be done. And this is an issue that can lead to destruction of a team. As Amanda explains, the folks in her cybersecurity department trust one another:

Amanda: While our department has multiple tracks, we're not siloed. It's still important for everyone in the department to be apprised of all the different projects, issues, and incidents to ensure that we're covering all our bases, this also provides the opportunity for different perspectives, and so we're all in the know, in the event the user or someone at the C-level asks us a question. It's about collectively being our best for the protection of the organization.[13]

Cybersecurity teams must trust one another—to be transparent, to be updated, and to do their best to "protect the organization." How does this relate to hiring? Certainly, you don't want your CSO in fear of losing his or her job, particularly for things which are beyond anybody's control. And that's a matter of good leadership working to create a high functioning corporate culture. But what you also want is a CSO to be concerned about the security of the company, damn the personal consequences. And that means two things: First, you actually need to have a person with the behavioral characteristics which drive them to do what's right. Someone with the attitude, "Company first, me second." They must have ethics, and we address that in the next section of this chapter. Second is making sure you have a person who's not worried about their ability to fix anything that's broken or to clean up any mess, no matter how bad. The behavioral characteristic missing here was self-confidence. Michael Woodson has a laser-focused perspective:

Michael: Another trait I look for in potential talent is truthfulness. In IT, things happen. Someone can move code in production and issues can occur. I want to hear the truth … a mistake happened. I want to hear "Oops, I grabbed the wrong module," versus, "I don't know, somebody else must have done something." I want to be confident that a person will admit to moving the wrong set of code in production. In IT, we need truthful people. If not, they could send us running down the wrong path. I'm not going to fire a person for making a mistake and admitting to it. But I will ter-

---

13 A. Tilley, in discussion with the authors. July 02, 2020.

minate someone for lying about a mistake that they made. I don't want this type of person on our team. They need to be willing to say, "I'm not perfect."[14]

Do you really want a CSO who is anything other than one hundred percent confident that he or she can recover from a ransomware attack? Can you afford not to have that behavioral characteristic in your CSO? In your threat assessment team? Anywhere in your organization? You don't have to—all you need is a good set of behavioral questions and a hiring manager who knows how to conduct the interview. It is very simple, and should be one of the first questions asked: "Tell us about the last time you faced a ransomware attack? Who did you communicate with, and how did you focus on saving the company?" Because it's not "if", it's "when". Every cybersecurity team will face this crisis, so as Amanda put it: "How will you be your best for the protection of the organization?"

We suspect that Uber did not ask this question. We suspect the company did not identify the crucial behaviors necessary for its CSO to be successful in a crisis. And if Uber did, they certainly did not collect differential data on his behavioral characteristics. If it had, it would have easily been able to determine this guy was great when things were great, but in the face of personal risk, he would aggressively protect himself at the expense of everyone and everything around him. T.J. Harrington explains how government experience translates into the private sector "concern" or "mentality" of putting the company first:

> **T.J.:** I was coming from the government space where mission was more important, where it was about the name on the front of the jersey, not the name on the back of the jersey. I used to bring that up all the time in my interviews with candidates for Citi. In the end, it's about the corporation's success. It's about the organizational success. And I was looking for people who were willing to make the sacrifices necessary to put the organization first, which we saw at the Bureau all the time. And that's one of those questions

---

[14] M. Woodson, in discussion with the authors. July 20, 2020.

that I would have had in my interview package—to get them to articulate to me the sacrifices they have made in past jobs to ensure the success of their team or their organizations.[15]

The most important take-away is this: you can extract data which reveal the behaviors of everyone you interview so you can create your team and get on the vector to success. As T.J. continues:

T.J.: It is critical that we have the right people. It's critical that they play as a team. And so teamwork becomes an attribute that I've got to define for them. And then the technology is just a tools that leverages their ability and helps leverage their work and helps them to be successful. Some of the best companies that have had some of the darkest days in cyberspace have had good technology, but did not have great teams, or the right people working for them to manage.[16]

If you identify, in detail, the behavioral characteristics required for any job (including the CSO), then you can build behavioral question sets and conduct a behavioral interview which will extract the data you need to determine whether the person sitting across from you *Will* do the job you need done. Uber didn't, and paid the price for it.

Will and Ethics

If you accept that who you are drives what you do, and circumstances can impact what a person does, you'll also understand that some people perform well when things are fine, but they erode drastically when things go badly. On the other hand, some people are as calm under stress as they are when things are fine. This is really the intersection of *Trust* and *Will*, which is ethics. What really drives a person's behavior? Opinions vary, and we don't intend to do a deep psychological dive here, but we do have a simple point to make. Behavior is driven by values, and values are

---

[15] T.J. Harrington, in discussion with the authors. July 31, 2020.
[16] *Id.*

driven by ethics. Part of understanding what a person will do is revealed by understanding the nature of their convictions. And that means understanding their moral compass.

We've long known that the most effective anticorruption measure a company can have is to hire people who are not corrupt. And to get there, the hiring process must do more than seek alignment with company values. It should examine each candidate's moral compass. It is possible to interview for a moral compass and to differentiate for ethics. And really, you can't afford not to. One of the many good questions which reveal someone's moral compass is, "Tell us about a situation where an authority figure (parent, teacher, boss) wanted you to do something you thought was wrong. How did you respond? What did you do? How was the situation resolved?" Chapter 6 will discuss the process of what to listen for and how to ask follow-up questions, but this examination is key.

John Kolb takes the complexities of ethics and distills it down for use in cybersecurity hiring:

> **John:** I look for people that are first and foremost highly ethical. If you want to stay in *Catch Me If You Can*-type of mode then go find a job somewhere else, because I'm not going to waste my time with that. I want people that give me straight answers and are going to be very upfront about what they're doing, why they're doing it, and so on. I do think you want to find people that are good problem solvers, whether they have a degree or not. Do they know how to parse something apart, really think their way through it, and know which threads to really pull. How to triage across many issues requires someone that is very persistent.[17]

The reality is, people don't really make mistakes when it comes to acting in accord with their values. They may face unpleasant consequences which, in retrospect, they would like to have avoided, but at the time of the action, they always choose a course of action aligned with who and what they are. Regret, generally, is the bad feeling driven by unexpected

---

[17] J. Kolb, in discussion with the authors. July 28, 2020.

consequences, or more precisely, by a consequence which they expected to avoid, and not by a "mistaken" value judgment. As a result, you can know a person by the choices they make, because they choose in accord with their values. The point is: people engage in unethical behavior because they're unethical, and a lack of ethics can be revealed during a behavioral interview.

As with the Uber data breach, and in the aforementioned quote from John Kolb, there are certain key ethical components when working in the cybersecurity world. Will the candidate act with integrity? Will the candidate speak honestly? For Adam Lee, it's simple:

> **Adam:** Dominion is a core values company, so the business case for anything you want to do, you've gotta cite it back to core values like excellence and ethics—all of the things that impact company culture—that if you're not constantly reinforcing you'll lose. If you're highly qualified, but you show up and you're clearly not Dominion material in terms of how you answer these questions, how you represent your integrity and how you do those things, you're not getting a job, I don't care what your qualifications are.[18]

Generally, ethics is not simple. It's not just about whether a person lies, cheats, or steals; these things are important but they are also both binary and simple—you do these things or you don't; you're honest or you're not. Consequently, they are easily disposed of during the *Trust* phase. Ethics is more substantial, it's about right and wrong, it's about the values a person holds, which not only results in honesty but which also structures how a person interacts with a broad range of people in a variety of situations. That's why ethics won't be revealed in the *Trust* phase. The *Trust* phase, fundamentally, is about honesty, while ethics, moral compass, and the values upon which they are built are much deeper.

The key to understanding a candidate's ethics is to ask behavioral questions that bring out right and wrong, and examine, not just what the candidate's values are, but also how the candidate makes value judgments.

---

[18] A. Lee, in discussion with the authors. July 09, 2020.

In the cybersecurity context, this can mean looking at how a candidate performs when forced to choose between moving quickly and staying within an ethical framework. Such an inquiry requires a close examination of how a candidate adheres to values when the circumstances are difficult. This could be about the moment ransomware begins to spread across the network, when the process of "shutting it down" also requires obtaining authority and reporting it within the business and externally. Or it could be about whether and how to hold accountable the senior executive that refuses to use an encrypted VPN connection when working from home because of the "hassle."

But you need to ask the questions—and only a behavioral interview will get you there. Imagine sitting across from a regulator who is reviewing your response to a malware attack, or being under oath before a senate committee reviewing how your company responded to a data breach, and being able to articulate how you differentiated for moral compass during hiring.

Part of the key to ethics and building the moral compass into a business culture is to regularly reconsider and rethink values. The danger with codes of ethics is when it becomes dogma, merely a rubric to follow. When that happens, the values upon which ethics are based begin to lose meaning and start becoming rote. Values have to be continuously tested, not to the extreme, but stressed enough so you are reminded they are real and they have purpose. As we examined in the Uber case, part of ethics is how you prioritize yourself and your own interests against the interests of the business and against the interests of others. Never practicing these thought processes, and failing to keep your moral compass fresh, leads to disaster in the same way never having a fire drill leads to chaos when there's a fire.

It is vital to act ethically consistently, to execute according to your code regardless of consequence. This extends to the idea that part of ethics is pride: how you value your own behavior against how you value the behavior of others. It's the hidden problem with moral high ground; adherence for its own sake rather than adherence because it fosters the moral outcome. Paul Maurer explains the Montreat premise:

Paul: We approach the cyber problem with a Judeo-Christian worldview. It's how we seek to operate, and it's the framework of how we teach cyber ethics. It's not the only moral lane in the world, but it's our lane. And even people who wouldn't necessarily agree with our particular lane, or all the particulars about our lane, agree with the basic premise that you have to have people of ethics and character as cyber operators and leaders.[19]

We share Paul's optic regarding the importance of ethics in general, but his point about the interaction of people with differing moral codes is crucial. Own the lane where you operate, but recognize there are other lanes. Be careful of summarily dismissing those who don't share your specific ethical system, but rather seek to understand what they believe. Find common ground. Remember, people are predictable because everyone acts according to their values. Understand a person's values, their moral compass, and you can predict what they *Will* do. If you can find common ground, you can probably find a way to build a trust relationship with a person even if you do not share an ethical code or deeper moral common ground. The key is never to presume they will act in accord with your values, but rather that they will act in accord with their own.

---

[19] P. Maurer, in discussion with the authors. July 13, 2020.

CHAPTER 6

The Interview

Before we get to the details of conducting the actual interview, it's important to review the preparation you need to have done to this point. Without having worked through *Can* and *Trust*, you won't have properly filtered the initial candidate pool down to those whom it is worth your time (and theirs) to interview, and the interview will be ineffective because you won't be interviewing the candidates most likely to succeed in your company. Interviewing people from a correctly refined candidate pool is crucial for a successful behavioral interview. In addition, without having clearly delineated what behavioral characteristics correlate to Success, Failure–Coachable, and Failure–Noncoachable, you won't be able to construct the correct behavioral question sets and will fail to differentiate candidates based on willingness to perform the job you need done. Properly done, behavioral interviews take time, so they should not be broadly used for large candidate pools. They should only be used for final differentiation, as this is the final phase of the *Can–Trust–Will* model. Austin Berglas illustrates his role in the interview process:

Austin: I think the biggest hurdle for candidates is getting to the interview phase. For me, that's where I separate the wheat from the chaff. I had an open posting for a cybersecurity analyst position, and it was directly underneath my lead penetration tester, a vulnerability specialist. So I posted it, and within say four days, I had about 140 candidates. And the difficulty is, I don't have the time—and my team doesn't have the time—to interview all 140 people. We'll get through the ones that are completely unqualified, we'll cut through those. For me, if you get to the interview stage, the way I'll do it is I'll have my lead person do the first interview, then I'll have somebody else on the team do an interview who is completely separate from that job role, and then if that candidate passes muster, and it appears to be a super great candidate, I'll interview him. And I'm not interviewing them for technical capabilities; I'm interviewing them for all of the other issues: can they speak properly, are they presentable, do they have the drive to want to learn, are they just looking to punch their ticket and move on?[1]

Not only does Austin describe a process which tracks the strategy of *Can–Trust–Will* by quickly and efficiently filtering the broad candidate pool into a refined and more manageable pool of initially qualified candidates, he has the discipline to act as the filter for the *Will* component—he takes over the behavioral interview aspect. He specifically rejects the temptation to interview for technical capability. Part of the reason is that he has built a trust culture, so he relies on his team to have done the *Can* work—he's confident they won't send him anyone who doesn't have the correct technical skills. And he also recognizes that if he's not disciplined in this way, the whole system breaks down. John Kolb has a similar strategy:

John: I think it's surprising when people get to have an interview like that with me because they expect that I'm going to ask the really hard technical question that they don't have an answer to, and I usually tell them, "Look, relax. Other people are going to make the decision on whether to hire you. I just want to know who you are." And that's incredibly important to me. And so is whether they bring different perspectives. Diversity is an important issue to me—so, are you bringing a different thought process or life experiences to the table, versus the people that are already here, so you can complement that. Those things are the types of questions I ask when I meet somebody. And I like them to talk about themselves—what they've done in their lives and what they're passionate about and so on, and that tells me quite a lot

---

[1] A. Berglas, in discussion with the authors. June 30, 2020.

about how they'll fit into the team, and how they'll be successful at Rensselaer.[2]

John's point is crucial. Diversity is necessary for a variety of reasons. Most important: high-performing teams are made up of different perspectives, approaches, and ways of thinking. John specifically conducts his behavioral interviews to ensure he knows what each candidate's life experiences and perspectives are so he can assemble a diverse, and therefore high-functioning, team. In addition, he avoids the legal issues which can follow from a poorly-designed hiring process. If you don't adequately structure the behavioral interview to ensure it differentiates for the capabilities you actually need, it will become a generic personality assessment and may open you to lawsuits from failed candidates (still, remember to always speak with an attorney—be it your in-house or outside counsel, or otherwise—before finalizing your behavioral question sets).

Generic personality assessments are often implemented through testing and are subject to two high-impact flaws. First, behavioral tests only assess general personality traits and consequently miss behavior-based indicators which demonstrably correlate with job performance. In essence, it's a judgment of whether a person can do the job but fails to assess whether the specific candidate being tested will do the job you need done. We addressed the importance of this distinction earlier. Second, since tests are provided by vendors, the generic personality traits they test for most often do not correlated with success in the particular job role at your company. The closest this type of test will get is to identify personality traits which their survey research has identified to be relevant to general notions of "success" or even survey-based data which proposes that particular traits are indicative of success in a given industry.

Developing Question Sets

There are several ways to get to know a candidate—depending on what you really want to know, of course. When it comes to actual behaviors, the interview can attempt to set up a real-time scenario where the candidate

---

[2] J. Kolb, in discussion with the authors. July 28, 2020.

must confront a massive data breach, with PR reps running wild, and sirens blaring. Would that be helpful? Sure. Is it practical? No. So how can actual behaviors truly be identified without setting the candidate off into a customized virtual disaster zone? The next best option is tailored behavioral question sets, which are designed to reveal whether a candidate has the behavior characteristics you have identified as correlating to successful job performance. Again, this is based on the well-established principle that past behavior is the best indicator of future behavior. In addition, it recognizes that it is much easier to accurately analyze a story than it is to analyze a highly prepared answer. The key to behavioral interviews is to ask questions designed to draw stories of the past from each candidate. Andrea Markstrom's approach is holistic:

> **Andrea:** During interviews, I'll always ask them a few questions generally focused on situational behavior. Tell me about a situation where this happened, or that happened—but what I'm looking for are individuals who, when faced with a crisis, how do they approach that? Do they go in and do they have their hair on fire? Or is it a calm, collected approach—what is their thinking pattern when they go into a critical situation? Because the most important thing—let's just say hopefully this will never happen, but if we were in the midst of a breach situation—the worst thing that can happen is IT has their hair on fire. And it is about how do you maintain that cool, calm approach in a crisis situation. So I ask during the interview: explain an example and how did you handle that. So that's one very important skill set. The other piece is tell me about a time where you made a mistake, and how did you handle that, and how did you communicate it?[3]

All of Andrea's questions are behavioral in nature because they ask for descriptors and not statements. It is critical to understand that behavioral question sets are not standard interview questions. Standard questions fail. They fail because they do not reveal anything about the candidate's

---

[3] A. Markstrom, in discussion with the authors. June 24, 2020.

willingness to do the job. Asking, "Why are you interested in working here?" will get you an answer, often a well-prepared and good-sounding answer. But it's not useful in the hiring process because having a good reason for wanting the job does not correlate to good job performance. Adam Bricker asks pointed questions which highlight the candidates' "mental models" and decision-making processes:

> **Adam:** I would also ask candidates and staff questions specific to the really important cybersecurity positions (looking for what they know, and do they know what they don't know; looking for collaboration examples). Finally, I ask them to define a situation where they faced a "cloud" where they have to progress through a tenuous situation where they cannot safely see the other side. I have them talk me through their mental model, their decision-making process, their fears, their joys. These situations include a start-up, climbing an unknown mountain in bad weather, dealing with a complex and unpleasant interpersonal situation, a complex incident response, etc. In each, I'm looking for that ethical dilemma and how they thought through it.[4]

Inherently, Adam's questions seek insight into how each candidate processes ambiguity and how they troubleshoot and problem solve when they know they don't have all the facts. In addition, his question elicits descriptions of how a candidate has exercised persistence and previously handled the emotional rollercoaster of working through a stressful experience. Nowhere in the answer will the candidate simply state what they are willing to do, but by listening carefully, Adam reaps a wealth of data about what the candidate most likely *Will* do in similar future situations.

To do this as effectively, as Adam does, requires the use of behavioral questions, those which generally begin with, "Tell us about a time when …" or "Describe for us a situation where you … ." By asking for stories about previous experiences, the candidate can't prepare textbook answers, and you don't fall into the trap of thinking that a candidate who

---

[4] A. Bricker, in discussion with the authors. July 13, 2020.

"interviewed well" will perform well on the job. Rodney points out how government agencies are also looking at parts of the interview process as an opportunity to allow candidates to illustrate what they can accomplish:

> **Rodney:** Even as we review applications for jobs, we don't just look at the degree, and those tried and true credentials, but we are thinking through the interview process and the selection process to find a better way for learners to demonstrate their capabilities or what they can accomplish what they can do and what they can accomplish.[5]

Viewing the behavioral interview as a method to truly understand what a candidate who *Can* do the job actually *Will* do once in a job is critical. And Rodney's focus on what the candidate can demonstrate, rather than what the candidate can say, is what keeps the interview on track. Only behavioral questions which trigger stories of previous events can demonstrate how the candidate responded and will reveal the deeper values which drive behavior and which otherwise would remain hidden. Once you have the behavior characteristics which correlate with success for your job properly categorized, and the behavioral question sets properly structured, you will be well on track to extracting the data you need to make better hiring decisions with confidence.

Developing question sets is a specific skill which usually requires expertise. To illustrate, we had a client who needed new hires to have a high level of both perseverance and initiative. Two of the five questions we delivered were as follows:

- Tell us about a time you set a goal that nobody thought you could achieve. How did you handle the situation? What was the outcome?
- Tell us about a time when you did more than was required on your own initiative. Specifically, how did you come to decide to do more, how did you decide what to do, and how did you deal with acting without permission?

---

[5] R. Petersen, in discussion with the authors. July 28, 2020.

These questions are difficult to develop because it requires expertise and practice to frame a question which will trigger a story that
reveals what you need to know, or even better, will lead to a conversation which reveals deeper insight into the candidate's character. Based
on the four model job roles we developed and presented in Chapter 5,
we have created corresponding *Will* question sets. These are available
in Appendix A. Additionally, we have included behavioral question sets
related to certain specific behaviors and included those in Appendix B
for reference.

Starting the Interview: Setting the Stage for Something Completely Different

At this point, you've done the preparation, you've correctly identified the
candidates to interview, and your behavioral question sets are prepared.
What now? The first phase of the interview is preparing the candidate
for what you need him or her to do—which is to dig deep for insightful and relevant stories. Behavioral interviews are not easy for either the
interviewer or the candidate, but it's important to emphasize this is not
a game of "gotcha." Remember, you are not looking for a candidate who
interviews well. You are looking for a candidate who has a history of actually performing the behaviors you need for the job you are filling. Consequently, part of your job as the interviewer is to help the candidate dig
deep for relevant stories. And that job starts with letting him or her know
what the interview is about, what you will be doing during the interview,
and most importantly, why.

An example of the introduction to the interview might run something
like this:

> Thank you for coming to interview with us. We are a high-quality
> team and we spend a lot of time and effort to find people we think
> can succeed here. We know it's not for everyone, and that's why
> we do this interview. We want to learn more about you.
>
> To do that, we have some questions we would like you to talk
> about that will require some thought, but that help us understand
> whether or not this will be a good fit moving forward.

We know it's difficult being interviewed like this, and we appreciate you being here and going through this process. And we are excited to get to learn more about you as a person. Are you ready to begin?

A more direct version of this introduction might run something like this:

Thank you for coming to interview with us. We are a high-quality team, and we spend a lot of time and effort to find people we think can succeed here. We know it's not for everyone, and that's why we do this interview. We want to learn more about you.

To do that, we have some questions we would like you to talk about. And while we want you to be comfortable, we also recognize that sometimes the best replies come when you're stressed. In fact, sometimes we learn a lot just by seeing which question topics are stressful! Please be assured we're not going to intentionally provoke you or anything like that, but some of this stuff is difficult and should make you feel uncomfortable. We just want you to know we're not being intentionally rude. But we are trying to learn about you from how you respond.

So again, we know this is difficult, and we appreciate you being here and going through this process. And we are excited to get to learn more about you as a person. Are you ready to begin?

Some might object to having a written introduction for being so formal and formulaic to the point where it interferes with building the rapport necessary to conduct the interview. The criticism is fair, but there are important reasons for using a template. First, it keeps the interviewer on track. The most significant cause of failure is an interviewer who becomes enamored with a charismatic candidate. Notwithstanding all of the time and effort which goes into planning a behavioral interview, we are all human. And the reason The Big Mistake exists is because it is so very easy to default to it. Second, it also serves to pull the candidate away from their prepared answers. Most candidates will have done a good deal of preparation for the interview, so it's only fair to let them know up front that the path to success is to trash their notes and their memorized answers, and to speak from the heart. Additionally, it's helpful to offer a sentiment like: "This is also your opportunity to evaluate (company name) based on what we ask and how we engage with you. Since you'll be working with me if hired, I encourage you to learn about me while I'm learning about you."

Finally, using a script for the initial stage helps demonstrate that all candidates were treated equally. Litigation from failed candidates is growing across all industries and simply must be considered during the behavioral interview process, and to remind the interviewer this is a focused conversation and not a feel-good exercise.

There are two additional items worth mentioning at this point. As you begin asking the behavioral question sets, always keep in mind you are evaluating the data given in the responses under the Failure–Coachable, Failure–Noncoachable, and Success assessment structure. This will keep you on track to make a candidate assessment which correlates to job performance. Beware if your thoughts begin tending toward, "What a great answer!" or "I really like this candidate!" The second is that while you should have writing materials to jot down a reminder or a particularly impactful thought during the conversation, the interviewer should never also be the notetaker. One person cannot effectively listen, evaluate, and ask follow-up questions, while also recording the interview content. Record the interview for later transcription or have a notetaker present to record what was said. The last thing you want is to miss an opportunity to dig for a truly revealing story because your train of thought was interrupted by writing down what was just said.

Conducting the Interview

After the introductory statement is done, the interview itself begins. This is a sometimes lengthy process of asking the question sets and interacting with the candidate through follow-up questions and facilitating discussion to ensure the best and most relevant stories are revealed in the interview process. The key here is to listen closely to how the candidate responds and to evaluate all of the data revealed by the candidate: some answers will reveal unexpected depth, and some will reveal a lack of depth. And while the content of the answer will provide a wealth of behavioral information, there is a large volume of additional data available in the context of the answer as well.

Behavioral interviews are not simply interviews to extract basic information. When I ask you, "Tell me about a time of highest stress in your life, and what you did to deal with it," evaluating the answer to that question is in layers. If you tell me about a time where the heel on your shoe broke and you missed a flight, well, I'm interested to know how you dealt with that stress—but I also need to be aware that breaking a heel and missing a flight is your concept of the highest-stress event in your life. This could be opposed to, "I was in my last semester of grad school, and my grandmother got hit by a car two weeks after my grandfather was diagnosed with Alzheimer's, I was the only one available so I quit school and moved across the country, and took care of my grandparents in the last eighteen months of their lives." That is a different level of stressful event. And so when you're evaluating behavioral questions, you have to understand what is being revealed, not only in the content of the answers but also in how the applicant is choosing to answer the question. This can help decide how the candidate *Will* function in the job.

Some candidates might be reluctant to share the stories you need. They may reply that it's too personal and they are uncomfortable sharing. While that reply itself may be valid, the key to differentiating candidates is to consider what the reply reveals. It may indicate a person who is not open or trusting, or perhaps someone who is insecure. It may indicate someone who cannot form relationships quickly or who may have difficulty trusting others. None of these possibilities are disqualifying, but they do give insight into the candidate's personality. Not in an absolute respect (i.e., open people are better) but in a differential data respect: are you looking for someone who is very private, or someone who is very open? This provides a foundation for your assessment of what the candidate will do during the workday. Again, the key differentiator revealed in a correctly-executed behavioral interview is to extract the behaviors each candidate is most likely to actually perform (*Will*) and to differentiate those behaviors from those the candidate is capable of performing, but not likely to actually engage in the ordinary course of the day (*Can*). And that helps you build an understanding of who the candidate is—which is what you need to know before a correct hiring decision can be made.

Alexi remembers being asked questions that attempted to investigate her behaviors:

> **Alexi:** My boss who interviewed me, from what I remember he kept asking me why I wanted to work at BlackBag and I said I got into this industry because I wanted to help people. And what better way to help people than teaching people on how to enhance their skills and understanding of forensics and our tools. He said the main reason he hired me was because of my personality, and the fact that I never changed my answer when he asked that question and he could tell I genuinely want to help people![6]

The ability to successfully answer behavioral questions is usually tied to storytelling. Some candidates may not tell stories well, and hopefully, our response to this circumstance is not a surprise at this point—it's not a disqualifier, it's a differentiator, which depends on the behavioral characteristics which correlate to Success, Failure–Coachable, or Failure–Noncoachable for the job role in your company. Thus, everything the candidate does during the interview is behavior, and every behavior can be assessed and mapped against the behavioral characteristics you structured when preparing for the interview. It doesn't matter where the behavior comes from. A story describing previous behavior is as revealing as actual behavior during the interview.

Spotlight: Gosh, I Don't Know!

What if your interview subject simply doesn't have an answer? A few years ago, we were interviewing candidates for an analytic job role in a very large company. During a day of interviews, we had two candidates who responded to the struggle to find stories in very different ways. Our first candidate was a young lady who came into the interview focused and highly prepared. She had a stack of reference materials and filled the room with energy—until we introduced the behavioral interview. Upon understanding none of her preparation would be useful, her despair was

---

[6] A. Michaels, in discussion with the authors. July 03, 2020.

evident, but she also appeared to decide to soldier on. And then we asked the first question. She paused for a minute and then blurted out, "Gosh, I don't know!"

Our second candidate could not have been more different. An obviously experienced middle-aged man came into the interview with a calm and practiced ease. He used very effective technique to build rapport and showed little concern when we introduced the behavioral interview. But over the course of nearly an hour, he simply refused to share any stories or reveal any behavioral data about himself. And he did so with a high level of skill. To every behavioral question, he replied with some version of "Well, it's not really a story, but ..." and then would recite a wonderful sounding statement of his capabilities. After he left the room when the interview was over, the trainee who was observing stated how impressive the candidate was, "What a great interview! He had perfect answers for everything!"

It wasn't until the trainee also listened to our analysis that he understood that the candidate had merely confirmed everything recited in his resumé but that we knew virtually nothing about him as a person. We knew all about his *Can* but nothing about his *Will*. He simply did not provide behavioral answers and he did it with great skill. The only thing we were certain he would actually do if he was hired was to speak eloquently about absolutely nothing at all. Our trainee had made The Big Mistake! We evaluated him as Failure–Noncoachable and recommended that he not be hired.

In contrast, our first candidate received a recommendation to hire with an evaluation of Failure–Coachable and a draft onboarding plan based on how she responded after her initial, "Gosh, I don't know!" As experienced interviewers, we took it as a signal to start exploring and to start helping her dig back through her memory. Starting with "emotional first aid" (a technique you'll learn in any quality interviewing course), we reassured her that her response was actually a great start and we went straight to the next question in the set. We prompted her to think back to events and activities outside what she might consider to be "work-related" experience; we reiterated that part of what makes stories come to the surface is taking a minute to think and that there was no penalty for sitting in silence beyond what would otherwise be normal in an interview to collect her thoughts. After about ten minutes of conversation and thinking, she began to brighten up and the stories flowed. "Oh, you know what? That happened to me in summer camp!" and, "That reminds me of when I was riding my bike across the country." She would never have made the connections or found the stories without facilitation, but with facilitation she was able to reveal to us key behavioral characteristics upon which we were able to evaluate her for success (or, in this case, Failure–Coachable) in our client's job role. This interaction gave us two things: one, her stories, and two, insight into how she problem-solved and how she responded to something unexpected and consequential. The man we gave a no-hire recommendation was unwilling to change in the face of something new. He was Failure–Noncoachable.

The process of facilitating the search for an answer to a behavioral question shows how the candidate is likely to interact with others when employed. A candidate's willingness to engage in the interview conversation with you to find stories also demonstrates how the candidate responds to guidance and suggestions. And in some ways, it's a window into how the candidate handles a stressful situation, even if it's just trying to answer an interview question. Even if it's not an "I don't know" answer, but it's a story which doesn't really provide much, and in some cases, the interviewer must press the candidate for more detail or for a more significant example. How the candidate responds to being pressed and whether more relevant examples are revealed are additional components of the final analysis.

A key component of the interview process to continuously keep in mind is this is not a game of "gotcha." Scrupulously avoid finding some kind of success in stumping the candidate during the behavioral interview. If a candidate cannot think of a story, that's the time to assist the candidate. You are not evaluating the candidate for his skill in having or finding stories. And you shouldn't really be interested in whether he tells stories well (unless that's a behavior which correlates to success in the job). You should focus on discovering her track record of behavior. When a candidate struggles to recall a story which answers the question you've posed, help her dig.

At the other end of the spectrum, some candidates will have no hesitation in launching into a story. That's neither good nor bad, it's just another factor to consider. The type of story the candidate shares and how they characterize it can also reveal a good deal about the candidate's personality. For example, a candidate whose "most stressful experience" was missing a connecting flight is likely to be a very different person from the candidate who shares the story of moving across the country for a year to give end-of-life care to a grandparent. Again, there is no correct answer. Rather, it's the type of story and how it's told which reveal characteristics of the candidate's personality. Once you have an understanding of who the candidate is, correlating the personality to the success/failure factors of the job role your company needs to have done becomes more straight-forward. Amanda has learned how her team functions, how she functions within it, and why certain behaviors benefit her team, in all of their roles:

> **Amanda:** For information security, we can't just hide in our corner and review logs all day. A really vital component for our success is being able to communicate, especially under high pressure sit-uations. As I previously mentioned, during the interview process, we take into account various factors before making a decision, including how a candidate responds during the white boarding session. Something my boss always likes to say is you know some-one's true colors when they are under stress. Information security will have to communicate with other departments: it is critical to our survival and our success. So we need to know that no matter what role you have in information security, you are going to be able to handle yourself in a potentially high pressure situation; you may need to communicate the issue, collect information from users as part of an investigation, or work with third parties to resolve an incident.[7]

Now, how to dig in and find those behaviors that you need? Just as developing the actual behavioral question sets is a learnable skill which requires expertise and practice, the same is true of the interview itself. A good starting point for understanding how behavioral questions

---

[7] A. Tilley, in discussion with the authors. July 02, 2020.

work and to prepare for conducting your first behavioral interview is to review and become familiar with the sample questions sets in appendices A and B. Based on our interviews with industry experts, our experience and expertise with behavioral interviews, and analysis of the NICE Cybersecurity Workforce Framework, the appendices contain common cybersecurity behavioral characteristics and sample question sets which will extract differential data for those behaviors. Working through the appendices will trigger your thinking, both regarding how the interview should be managed and in developing behavioral questions which are more finely tuned to your needs. That's the point—the appendices are provided as a jumping-off point for you.

We also recommend that you take some training in interviewing. Again, this is a learned skill, but it is a skill everyone should have. The simple truth about interviewing is it's a skill which can only be developed through practice, and that means role-playing. Particularly, in HR departments or recruiter firms, ongoing practice in interviewing is crucial to effectively extracting differential data in a behavioral interview. This book is devoted to the process of how to identify, winnow, and select the employees you need for cybersecurity roles in your company. And while interviewing is a crucial part of the process, it's a complex enough skill to warrant a separate volume. Even if you don't regularly conduct interviews yourself, you simply must know enough about interviewing to be able to evaluate the skill level of those in your company who do.

As mentioned earlier, how a candidate responds to the digging process is revealing and should be a part of the assessment you do both during and after the interview. For the interviewer, switching from setting up and asking the behavioral question to an open-ended elicitation is a critical part of the behavioral interviewer's skill set. Having the ability to conduct both a behavioral interview and an open-ended elicitation to support the behavioral questions is important. That's why interview training and practice, whether through role-playing or by conducting many interviews, is crucial to success.

What you should care about, the thing you need to accurately assess a candidate, is good stories which address the behavioral question sets identified in your job description. Be willing to take any path which gets you to good stories. Any path which prevents you from getting to good stories is a blind alley to be avoided. Through experience, Adam Bricker has developed his own strategy for approaching the behavioral interview:

> **Adam:** While building my professional practice and hiring staff all over the world while serving in a humanitarian aid organization, I learned to ask the questions in an "orthogonal" way. Not, "Are you a good athlete?" Not, "Are you smart?" But answer to ask, "Describe to me a situation in your life where you proactively, of your own volition, put yourself in harm's way just because you thought it was fun, and describe a situation in that field where you had to navigate through a 'fog bank' of decision-making—you had to get to the other side without any clear path." I use that question to this day, and with extremely rare exceptions (sometimes they still don't get along well with other people—there's a required team dynamic there), it has literally never failed. Also, that turns out to be a pretty interesting question to leverage on cybersecurity interviews as well.[8]

This deeper dive allows Adam to find that concrete grasp of candidate behaviors. John Kolb describes his approach:

> **John:** I'm very intentional in the questions I ask, but I'm not necessarily looking for direct answers or "yes or no" answers. I am looking for something that teases out somebody's character and personality a little bit. And once again, how ethical do I think this person is, will they stand in the wind if something comes up that's against where they might want to go or where they think there's a problem.[9]

The final observation about conducting the behavioral interview is that the order of questions is often irrelevant. In fact, sometimes jumping between question sets or moving on temporarily from a question which is not lending itself to a story can be a good way to "shake things loose"

[8] A. Bricker, in discussion with the authors. July 13, 2020.
[9] J. Kolb, in discussion with the authors. July 28, 2020.

and open new trajectories for the candidate. The reason question sets are used, rather than just one question for each behavioral characteristic, is to keep your focus on the stories—and therefore the candidate, rather than on the questions. The key is to understand the candidate through good, deep, relevant stories for each behavioral characteristic you have identified in your job description. The interview should end only when you have enough data, or it is evident that a story will not be forthcoming for one or several behavioral characteristics. You're looking for a candidate who demonstrates the behaviors you need, you are not looking for a candidate who just interviews well.

Spotlight: Who Interviews?

Standard interviewing is a learned skill. It's the process of directing a conversation with the purpose of extracting information from the person being interviewed. It takes practice, and you're going to get it wrong before you can get it right. And behavioral interviewing is a step deeper. It's still a purpose-driven conversation, but rather than extracting information, the behavioral interview extracts demonstrations of previous behavior from the person being interviewed. The bottom line is you have to know how to interview, and that means get trained and then practice, practice, practice. We make this point for a deeper purpose: the companies that make the best hiring decisions always have the hiring manager be a part of, if not fully conduct, the behavioral interview.

At a minimum, the hiring manager needs to observe each interview, but the best practice is for hiring managers to learn how to conduct behavioral interviews, and to do the interviews themselves before making the hiring decision. Why? Because hiring is a consequential decision. If you are interviewing somebody and hiring them to go work for somebody else, you are very likely to evaluate candidates differently than if you are hiring candidates who are going to work for you. Holistically, the interview needs to be done by a person who's going to be impacted consequentially by the hire—this could be the candidate's (potential) direct boss, but it can also include the team members that will work with the (potential) new hire as well.

Why is this important? Because, as we've mentioned in previous chapters, interviews are where biases most easily show up, because interviewers who are not adequately trained and prepared often decide on the fly what to ask of whom and how to interpret the answer. Everyone knows some executive who is absolutely certain he knows the one question that will really predict good candidates ("If you were stranded on a desert island …"). The Big Mistake, anyone? And there are also studies available which have researched interviews for elite positions, such as those in professional services firms, and concluded that hobbies, particularly those associated with the rich, feature prominently as a selection criterion. Hiring officials simply must learn how to conduct behavioral interviews that extract data which actually correlate with job performance. The *Can–Trust–Will* process can help executives understand why their "one question" system fails so often, and that learning how to interview is the key to effective hiring and low employee turnover.

This includes interviews that focus on assessing "fit with our culture," which is the number one hiring criterion employers report using, according to some surveys. And by this time, we already know why this is on the road to The Big Mistake—because it's one of the squishiest attributes to measure. Few organizations have an accurate and consistent view of their own culture—and even if they do, understanding what attributes represent a good fit is not straightforward. The generic notion of "fit with culture" simply does not correlate to job performance.

For example, does the fact that an applicant belonged to a fraternity reflect experience working with others or does it reflect elitism or does it indicate misogyny? Should it be completely irrelevant? The answer for this example lies in whether "belonging to a fraternity" correlates to job performance. We predict it does not correlate at all—we'd be surprised to learn it predicts behavior of any kind, positive or negative. It simply requires deeper analysis. Letting someone with no experience or training make such calls is a recipe for bad hires and, of course, discriminatory behavior. But it may be helpful, especially for smaller teams, to have a few of the potential new hire's colleagues sit in. Martin Durst expressed agreement with this idea:

Martin: I think it's important for the group to sit in on interviews so that we can get a feel for the potential teammate, and let our opinions be heard.[10]

Many organizations follow this approach. The team as a unit may offer important insights, as Marie Chudolij points out:

Marie: When you're working with smaller, tight-knit organizations or really just smaller groups, they tend to understand the need for the team to be a cohesive unit. That's where they are going to have more understanding for other folks to be involved. You know, it's not necessarily how a traditional hierarchy works, where only the manager or director is able to make these decisions. It's a team decision. If they're hiring a new director or manager that I am going to report to, and I didn't get along with that person, that could pull the whole team apart.[11]

The key here is to understand that the purpose of the interview is to extract differential behavioral data, and nothing should be allowed to interfere with accomplishing that goal. Having observers is fine, especially if one of the relevant behavioral characteristics is the ability to perform under pressure. Being the focus of attention in a consequential environment full of strangers could certainly be revealing. In addition, we have found it is useful for people learning the behavioral interview process to observe behavioral interviews. It can also assist current members of the team to observe, as part of providing input for the new hires, onboarding program. Still, it is important to set boundaries which should include identifying to the candidate the reason for all the nonspeaking people in the room. And finally, while there may be an egalitarian desire to "let everybody ask a question," we find this practice does little to improve the outcome and only makes the interview more cumbersome.

---

[10] M. Durst, in discussion with the authors. June 29, 2020.
[11] M. Chudolij, in discussion with the authors. July 24, 2020.

Spotlight: Ending the Interview

Asking for candidate questions at the end of the interview is a waste of time. Many of our clients are initially offended at this advice, and from an egalitarian perspective, their reaction is well-taken. The reasons we give this advice begins with the reality that the practice doesn't reveal anything useful, and it starts you down the road to The Big Mistake. Candidate questions don't reveal differential data because they are usually crafted in advance so that the candidate can create rapport, show interest, and demonstrate how well she has prepared for the interview itself. It's irrelevant to the behavioral interview. You're both mentally drained (as you should be) and now we're going to talk about hours, pay and dress code? All of that can be addressed during contract negotiations with the candidate who gets the job offer. Additionally, taking steps to "ensure the applicant is left with a positive impression of the interviewer and the organization," as some generally available advice recommends, is directly contrary to the purpose of the behavioral interview. The purpose is not to impress the applicant, it's to understand who the applicant is and how he is likely to behave in the future. Simply thank him for participating in such a difficult process and let him get on to the rest of his day while you get on to the next interview.

Analyzing the Interview

Once the interview itself is done, the analysis can begin. This is where you spend a few minutes reviewing the data revealed by the candidate's stories and make your final decision regarding whether to recommend offering the candidate a job. It does not matter if the analysis is done in a twenty-minute session after each interview and before the next, or if the last two hours of the day are blocked to conduct reviews on the interviews done that day. And it doesn't matter if the hiring manager conducts the interviews and analysis solo, or if the interviews are done with observers and the analysis is done by the group that was in the room. All that matters is that the behavioral characteristics demonstrated by the candidate's stories are structured into the list of behavioral characteristics prepared for the job role, and a final assessment is made for each one: Failure–Coachable, Failure–Noncoachable, and Success.

Obviously, Success behaviors support a hire decision, while Failure–Noncoachable behaviors support a no-hire decision. But what you will most often find is most candidates are Failure–Coachable. And we've mentioned this previously—it's actually pretty rare to find exactly the candidates you need, and that's why we've devoted a chapter to new employee onboarding. And since most candidates will be Failure–Coachable, most hiring decisions will be driven by complex factors such as training budget, and the differing levels of time and cost to address the different combinations of Failure–Coachable assessments. Consequently, post-interview analysis will focus on Failure–Coachable behaviors. Most of your candidates will be in this category, and the results will give a good indication of the training needed and the learning curve likely to be faced by a prospective employee. It is often a good idea to prepare and include in the hiring recommendation a first draft of the training and coaching the candidate will need to be successful during the onboarding process.

The easiest evaluations will be those candidates who have a high level of Failure–Noncoachable indicators. These are the quick "no" decisions, but there is a significant note of caution here. Failure–Noncoachable candidates should not be rejected from further consideration across the board. Rather, they should only be identified as not suitable for the specific job role the behavioral interview covered. To extract the most value from your resources, each candidate's behavioral interview results should be reviewed to determine whether another job, one with different behavioral characteristics, provides a suitable match for the candidate.

More obviously, candidates with high levels of Success indicators are very nearly to the point of being eligible for a job offer. The key with candidates who have high levels of Success indicators is to confirm they have low levels of Failure–Noncoachable indicators. A candidate with high levels of both Success and Failure–Noncoachable should be treated as if they only had high levels of Failure–Noncoachable, because Failure–Noncoachable behaviors have significantly more impact on the work environment than any other factor. In addition, candidates with high levels of Success indicators should also be reviewed for Failure–Coachable indicators to ensure an appropriate onboarding process is developed for that candidate. Just because they are on a success trajectory does not mean they should be ignored at onboarding.

Part of this process is to ensure that all question sets are asked during the behavioral interview. It's a mistake to stop an interview midway through because the candidate has provided Success indicator stories to that point. It's critical to ensure each candidate is evaluated across all behavioral characteristics. Missing one or two question sets can result in missing Failure–Noncoachable behaviors which lead to a bad hire. The exception is for a candidate who has a high level of Failure–Noncoachable indicators. If it's clear that the candidate will not be suitable for any job role in your company, continuing on to the bitter end is not worthwhile.

Most candidates or, more precisely, most successful candidates, will have Success indicators, almost no Failure–Noncoachable indicators, and a noticeable level of Failure–Coachable indicators. After all, we are dealing with people. Nobody is perfect, and everybody can improve. The trap which we have discussed previously is to insist on candidates who only have Success indicators and no Failure indicators. This is an unrealistic approach which not only dismisses the reality of people but also anticipates an effortless onboarding process based on the presumption that the perfect candidate will immediately become the perfect employee.

Onboarding is a crucial process which builds relationships, enhances communications, and develops high-performance work units over time through consistent interaction across the enterprise. A mindset which seeks perfect new hires is one which also anticipates perfect performance without effort or communication, and which necessarily devolves into frustration and dysfunction when things don't go perfectly—which is inevitable.

A correctly developed and executed behavioral interview will reveal the candidates who should be offered jobs. These candidates will be those who have measurable Success indicators, almost no Failure–Noncoachable indicators and sufficient Failure–Coachable indicators upon which to build an onboarding and new employee integration plan.

So Much Goes Into the Interview:
Here's a Summary

At this point, many of our clients become overwhelmed. They understand the preparation work that needs to be done before the behavioral interview, but the amount of work to be done after the interview is completed seems huge. And what about level setting? How do you ensure candidates who have been interviewed by different people in HR are treated equally? How can the hiring manager be assured all candidates have been evaluated the same? Let's re-emphasize a crucial point we made earlier in the book. The hiring manager simply must participate in the behavioral interview of all candidates. Even if the hiring manager is just an observer, neither conducting the interview nor taking the notes, it is the hiring manager who must be present to hear the stories told by every candidate, to make the final evaluation, and then to select the candidate who will be offered the job. There simply is no way around this.

Remain aware that The Big Mistake lurks constantly. Avoid falling into the trap of hiring a candidate based on some form of, "I like this guy." It really doesn't matter if the candidate is likable or if you had great rapport during the interview—"likability" is simply not relevant. Stay focused on whether the candidate demonstrates a history of performing the behaviors you need for the job you're filling and whether any deficits can be remedied through training. And never make the mistake of hiring someone because "they interviewed well." You're looking for someone who demonstrates a track record of ability and willingness to do the behaviors the job requires. Unless "interviewing well" is a part of your business model for which it makes sense for you to pay people, it's not relevant.

Remember that if a candidate gets nervous or uncomfortable sharing what they consider to be private information with a stranger, that tells you something about how they behave. Working with a person requires understanding who that person is—how can you possibly work with somebody if you don't know how they're going to respond or react? If a candidate is not willing to share themselves in an interview, they're not going to be willing to share themselves on the job. And if sharing yourself on the job is important because you will be working in a team environment, then that person may be better suited to the story of our delivery driver who is happiest alone, getting the job done, and not having to interact. In that case, you're not going to be all that concerned about a candidate not wanting to share the details. It all comes back around to what behavioral characteristics you're looking for. And all of the candidate's responses in the behavioral interview are factors which give you insight into the behavioral characteristics which correlate to job performance at your company.

As you gain experience conducting behavioral interviews, you'll get better at estimating the time you'll need. Initially, plan on ten to twenty minutes to introduce the candidate to the process and ten to fifteen minutes per question thereafter. Depending on the behaviors and the job you're filling, most basic behavioral interviews for entry-level jobs will go about two hours.

Much of the field of cybersecurity deals in unknowns. Whether you are talking threat vectors, zero-day exploits, rapidly evolving malware, new technological releases, and the latest requisite patches, there is always an element of the unknown. Gail Gottehrer refers to it as the gray zone:

> **Gail:** It's about being flexible enough to say, we work and live in an area that's all in the gray zone. No matter how many hours I work, I will not be able to anticipate everything (even though I want to). Lawyers and people in the cybersecurity field like to know that if we work hard enough and spend enough hours preparing, we'll know the question before it's asked and have the answer to every question that's asked. That doesn't work in cyber. It's an unattainable goal, so you need someone who can accept the fact that everything's gray—the unknown is going to happen no matter what you do; you have to be comfortable with uncertainty, and comfortable telling senior management that you don't have all the answers, but here's your best plan given what you do know, with the understanding that when you start doing an investigation into an alleged cyber incident, you know very few facts, and that what you infer from the facts you have may turn out to be wrong.[12]

One of the important aspects of this "gray zone," for many cybersecurity roles, is being able to be open about making mistakes. As Andrea Markstrom explains, it's about accountability and growth:

---

[12] G. Gottehrer, in discussion with the authors. July 09, 2020.

Andrea: I learn every day, I make mistakes every day—it's what we learn from it, and it's being humble, it's being open, it's being accountable—those are all very important skill sets to me in order to be a good team player. And to be able to learn. Because in order for you—or somebody on your team—to grow, they have to be open to learning, and they have to be open to feedback. And they have to also not be afraid to say, you know what, this is what happened, this is a mistake I made, but this is what I learned, I'm accountable, and move on. So that level of accountability and that level of being able to be responsible about it is super important.[13]

As Wheeler Coleman explains, he seeks out detail when discussing how people handle crises:

Wheeler: I look at whether I get a general answer versus a specific answer. I want to know whether a person will open up to me and give me an honest account of when they lost "their hair." For example, I want to know the details about a time when they lost their cool when somebody "pushed their buttons" the wrong way. I want to know exactly what happened, what they learned from that experience and how they reconciled the situation.[14]

They may reply that it's too personal and they may be genuinely uncomfortable sharing. While the reply itself may be valid, what does it reveal? It indicates a person who is not open or trusting, perhaps someone who is insecure. This may indicate someone who may not form relationships quickly or who may have difficulty trusting others. None of these possibilities are disqualifying, but they do give insight into the candidate's personality. And that helps you build an understanding of who the candidate is—which is what you need to know before a correct hiring decision can be made.

Some candidates may have difficulty thinking of a suitable story. This is an opportunity for the interviewed to engage in an open exchange with

---

[13] A. Markstrom, in discussion with the authors. June 24, 2020.

[14] W. Coleman, in discussion with the authors. August 12, 2020.

the candidate, a discussion about what the interviewer is looking for and a dialogue designed to assist the candidate to dig through memory to find a story which helps. These exchanges are useful because they often become structured conversations which show how the candidate is likely to interact with others when employed.

The type of story the candidate shares and how they characterize it can also reveal a good deal about the candidate's personality. For example, a candidate whose "most stressful experience" was missing a connecting flight is likely to be a very different person from the candidate who shares the story of moving across the country for a year to give end-of-life care to a grandparent. Again, there is no correct answer. Rather, it's the type of story and how it's told which reveal characteristics of the candidate's personality. Once you have an understanding of who the candidate is, correlating the personality to the success/failure factors of the job you need done becomes more straightforward. The key is to have proper question sets and to learn how to conduct the interview, so all relevant data are captured.

Ongoing analysis of a candidate's answers must also be performed by the interviewer during the interview to ensure proper follow-up questions are asked and the candidate's best possible stories are found. And a final analysis of the interview is necessary to properly structure differential data into Failure–Coachable, Failure–Noncoachable, and Success, to ensure an accurate hiring decision, and to inform the onboarding process.

CHAPTER 7

Onboarding Cybersecurity Hires (and Building Cybersecurity Into Onboarding)

You've built and executed the *Can–Trust–Will* hiring process and hired people who have the technical skill and behavioral characteristics which correlate with high performance in your company. All done? Not quite. Cybersecurity organizations operate as teams, no matter how large or small. And when a new member has been hired, proper onboarding is essential for success. Marie Chudolij describes the impact a new person can have:

> **Marie:** It comes back to teamwork. I've worked on teams where they have a great relationship, and they are unstoppable. Someone new may come in and it really can alter the team as a whole.[1]

She continues:

> **Marie:** You have to love your team and work well with them and you really need grit to get through the long hours and critical issues that pop up. To get through it, you need passion and perseverance. If you don't work with like-minded individuals, it's going to bring you down.[2]

---

[1] M. Chudolij, in discussion with the authors. July 24, 2020.
[2] *Id.*

The key here is to recognize that high performance begins with hiring people who will succeed at your company and continues with an equally high-performance onboarding process which integrates new hires into the team and the company. Bringing in good people and then cutting them adrift to find their own way has drastic consequences.

Shared Intention and Mission Statements

Many of the interviews we've conducted have led to a helpful conclusion surrounding onboarding: shared intention, often supported by mission statements, setup a foundational strategy for cybersecurity teams. Shared intention bonds teams and creates a sense of partnership and belonging. As Adam Lee explains, solid missions can help to keep a team together:

> **Adam:** Candidates are a BEAR to find. The good ones can hop ship. Companies are constantly competing for talent, and individuals with a strong cyber security skill set can move across sectors with it. The MISSION of our company—power company to the Pentagon, nuclear programs, pipeline projects, etc.—does help keep and attract candidates for us, so being able to tell the story, through the hiring process, of what cyber war you are fighting, and how they can make a difference to that battle is an important selling point.[3]

The selling point here is the sense of belonging. The old days of the loner "IT guy" are gone, but those days are gone for two reasons. First, companies need teams to be effective, but second, and even more important, people want to belong. Andrea Markstrom speaks about her team this way:

> **Andrea:** I want [the team's] input as to how we can change it together so that they feel a part of the team, and they're invested in it, but also so that they understand the "why" and create and

---

[3] A. Lee, in discussion with the authors. July 09, 2020.

share the vision. We, as leaders, need to set the stage and then let the team shine. As leaders, we let the team rise.[4]

That bears repeating: "As leaders, we let the team rise." Adam Bricker agrees:

Adam: I find that most of the really, really talented people I work with in cybersecurity are passionate about the "why" they serve.[5]

Part of creating a sense of belonging means having a process which integrates each new person into the whole. It's complex, but having a high-functioning, well-integrated team is essential. Adam Bricker found insight into the complexities when he asked one of the best ethical hackers in the world to describe what makes the hardest cyber defenses so difficult to penetrate:

Adam: He said the most effective (i.e., difficult for hackers) are those teams of cybersecurity professionals that work together as a team, as a collaborative team and keep changing their operations, tactics, designs, and roles. They're continuously changing their environments, continuously looking for something that's going to work because they created what it is today. They're consciously changing products, and then looking for what "unknown" (and thus a potential threat) changed in their environment relative to yesterday. You see those high-level AI-based tools engaged, but if you're just running those tools, as opposed to operating the environment and thinking about this holistic environment—the bad guys will get by. In the last seven years, the only one that they've not been able to successfully hack into on a regular basis was a financial services firm, because they effectively deploy and nurture the human element of cybersecurity.[6]

---

[4] M. Andrea, in discussion with the authors. June 09, 2020.
[5] A. Markstrom, in discussion with the authors. June 24, 2020.
[6] A. Bricker, in discussion with the authors. July 13, 2020.

Individuals working alone can no longer succeed in today's cybersecurity environment. It's too complex for solo operators, and it requires teams with what Adam calls "the human element." This is why an onboarding process must follow the hiring process. Integrated teams, those that share the intention to execute the mission, are essential to success in today's complex cyber world. And that should be the goal of your onboarding process. Solid mission statements that create shared intention and well-articulated answers regarding "why" the team exists are the foundation upon which company culture is built. Shared intention relies on interaction between people. And interaction is not just communication, nor is it just ethics. At its core, interaction means relationships. Onboarding should focus on building relationships within your team between the new hires and the experienced operators.

The key with onboarding is to build relationships, not skills. If there is skill training (and all of your Failure–Coachable new hires will be in skill training), then classes and other structured processes should be set up. But skill training is not onboarding. Neither is a facility tour, nor is a desk prepared with office supplies and a current edition of the HR manual. All of those things are useful and should definitely be done. But creating a login and reviewing the policy manual is not onboarding.

Successful teamwork is built on shared intention. Shared intention is driven by relationships. Consequently, the purpose of an onboarding program is to build relationships. Fostering shared intention begins with facilitating relationships. Even if a company has clearly articulated goals and objectives, merely including them in a handbook or in an onboarding email will not inspire employees to make it a priority. Creating a mission-oriented culture requires both clear purpose and strong relationships. T.J. Harrington explains how he learned the importance of mission-oriented mindset and how he carried that strategy through to Citi:

T.J.: I'll admit when I first got this job with Citi, I found the workforce and my early conversations to be a little bit challenging; I think it was trying to understand their mindset—it wasn't the same as what the paramilitary mission-oriented operation we'd had at the FBI. In the corporate culture, that mission discussion wasn't had very often. One of the surprising things was that they had goals and objectives everywhere, but not a real understanding of mission and commitment, what was expected. People would do things, meet the goal, and then stand there and wait for leadership to tell them then what's the next goal, or what's the next objective they've got to do. And that bothered me. So we began to try to think about how you instill the shared consciousness that you want your workforce to have. General McChrystal—I followed him around in Afghanistan for a period of time, back when we were in the Bureau, and I had the opportunity to watch him do a secure video teleconference with 1,000 people on it. And then you go into a corporate environment and you get ten or fifteen in a video conference and it deteriorates pretty quickly. You could see that there wasn't the discipline that we needed around having these discussions, as opposed to what McChrystal was able to do, which was to share commander's intent with 1,000-plus people in a video conference. Everybody then goes and executes their job, knowing what the boss wants and empowering them to actually do things, to actually take action, because you know you're going to be in the right because you understand what our mission is and what the boss wants you to do each and every day. And so for me at Citi, part of that was trying to develop a new battle rhythm for the organization.[7]

And that's the key: How do you instill the shared consciousness? How do you build a sense of belonging? How do you empower the team to do things in the absence of specific instructions? In cybersecurity, the need for team members to feel empowered to fulfill the mission, once it's defined, is critical. Michael Woodson elaborates:

Michael: I'm big on team empowerment. I have a close bond with my team members and I have them take responsibility for their particular verticals, whether it be security operations, cybersecurity engineering, identity access management, or risk management.

---

[7] T.J. Harrington, in discussion with the authors. July 31, 2020.

We make sure that everybody is pulling their weight. It's all about orchestration and collaboration.[8]

Allowing team members to take responsibility is a key component of building mission-focused leadership. It's a layered approach to creating the opportunity for responsibility and empowerment. As Adam Lee describes it:

Adam: It is essential to empower the cybersecurity team to OWN security in that often intimidating operational space, and view their role as client servicing.[9]

Adam's description goes back a few chapters but is important here as well. Part of the "why," part of belonging, is purpose. T.J. Harrington expands on this:

T.J.: One of the things I found interesting was that these cyber folks—they knew their portion of the job, but they forgot sometimes that they were working for a bank. So being able to tell them that we just did an IPO for some company, or that we just won some other competition for services for some big Fortune 500 company—they needed to remember that they're part of this business, and that the things that they are doing are helping to enable that business. Because I didn't see them understanding this idea that information security specifically is a business enabler. You're helping to create the opportunity for the business to be successful. And so, we would drive that home in our documents and in our discussions and every presentation that we made.[10]

You hired certain candidates because they have the behavioral characteristics which are needed to succeed at your company. Ensuring they

---

[8] M. Woodson, in discussion with the authors. July 20, 2020.
[9] A. Lee, in discussion with the authors. July 09, 2020.
[10] T.J. Harrington, in discussion with the authors, July 31, 2020.

become engaged with what the company does and then stay engaged with what the company does will keep turnover low and performance high.

The Onboarding Process

Even the perfect candidate can underperform as a new employee if onboarding is not conducted in a way which ensures success. Consequently, onboarding is not a separate function, nor is it transitional function. Rather, it's the final step in the hiring process. Effective employee onboarding is based on two key elements of human functioning. First, people need relationships, and second, people need to be appreciated for their contribution. The often-ignored part of this second point is people need to be positioned to make a contribution. What does this mean? Part of your onboarding program should be giving brand-new people challenges, small projects which are both necessary and achievable. Starting with small, attainable projects gives a new person the opportunity to achieve success, be recognized, and move forward to the next project. In addition, having new employees work with several different groups of people fosters the development of a variety of relationships while keeping their bandwidth full. This is the outline for a productive cycle of relationships, team integration, achievement, and recognition.

How does this actually work? First, let's look at relationships. Most companies perform onboarding by some sort of tour of the workspace, pro forma introductions to the others who inhabit the same area, and some version of access to company materials. This varies from a stack of reading the new employee finds at the workstation all the way to a series of classes, lectures, and webinars designed to teach the new person about the company. All of this is good, but it doesn't foster relationships.

At this point, some will say relationships develop over time and systems which attempt to team-build or otherwise push people together only result in artificial interaction, which is not useful because it's not genuine. True. And we strongly agree that conventional "team-building" programs are a waste of time and resources. But leaving new people to find their own way into working relationships is the path to failure for all but the few who are natural networkers. The key to onboarding is a program of consequential interactions; not "offsite" meetings or any of the other popular "team-building" exercises, but consequential projects of varying duration with different people.

Essentially, an effective onboarding program is an ongoing series of scheduled interactions between new employees and a broad range of personnel across the company. Creativity is the key to finding a system which works in your corporate culture, but the path to success is short, structured interactions where the new employee can observe the senior person perform their job, followed by a 10- to 15-minute conversation to build rapport and allow the new employee to ask questions about why the senior person took the action they were observed taking.

Spotlight: Just Shadow Me

Many companies, no matter the size, believe an important aspect of onboarding is the "shadowing" process. Typically, however, this just includes having a colleague in the same department or at the same level allow the new hire to accompany them for a few hours. This type of shadowing activity is well-intentioned, but doesn't get to the right result because while it leads to introductions, it does not foster relationships. In order to properly onboard a new cybersecurity hire, that person must spend time with a broad cross section of the company, within the cybersecurity team and more importantly across the business units. This type of learning and relationship building activity allows new hires to fully understand and appreciate the cybersecurity team mission, how shared intention functions across the organization as a whole, and how the business actually works. Andrea Markstrom describes her ongoing process:

> **Andrea:** I bring my team along with me, with the conversation. It's important to include them. And instead of me being directive and expecting my team to be order-takers, I shift that and turn to them for ideas, recommendations, solutions. They are empowered, they are part of the discussion.[11]

---

[11] A. Markstrom, in discussion with the authors. June 24, 2020.

And while Andrea's description is more about how she interacts with her team than it is about onbaording, the point remains. By making her team part of the conversation rather than just introducing them, the interactions are consequential and they build relationships. This process can take many forms, depending on the size and type of private business or government entity. But on the whole, the new hire should have the opportunity to meet and spend time with personnel across the business, while spending the most time with the representative employees from different layers of the cybersecurity team.

As an example, in a notional financial institution which has four business lines, a mid-level VP of finance has four meetings each week: one with the VP and top staff of each business line. Even though these are finance meetings, each new cybersecurity employee should be assigned to accompany the finance VP to one of these meetings as an observer during their onboarding process. To get a sense of what issues will be discussed at each meeting, each new employee is scheduled to meet the VP ten minutes prior to the assigned meeting to get briefly acquainted and learn about the meeting agenda. The new cybersecurity employee accompanies the VP to the meeting and then spends 10 to 15 minutes after the meeting in follow-up discussion. The new employee then returns to his or her regular work while the VP goes on to the next meeting accompanied by another new employee. When properly structured and scheduled, this system allows the VP to meet and spend a bit of time with all new cyber employees without having to find large blocks of time to build rapport with new staff. And the new cyber employees get to learn corporate culture by seeing all types of employees in action; they get exposure to a variety of company issues; and they get the chance to briefly interact with many of the more senior employees with whom they would otherwise not interact at all.

This example essentially describes a shadowing process but with significant differences. First, it puts the new employee in an actual business meeting which is a consequential environment where the work of the company is happening. Scheduling the interaction to coincide with a business meeting also avoids one of the pitfalls which are common to shadowing programs which merely block time on an executive's schedule. The key to relationships, to understanding the business, and to developing a sense of belonging is to see how the executive functions in the job role. Merely spending time near the executive for a few hours does not accomplish any of these purposes. Second, the interaction is structured to foster a relationship. Both the executive and the new employee know when the interaction begins and ends, and they both know what the topic of discussion should be. And it's the end time which is most significant. Busy executives are generally much more willing to share their time if they know it's a 15-minute interaction. Most executives actually don't have much control over their schedule and are wary of committing to an open-ended interaction. In addition, when the new employee also knows they'll have 15 minutes, the conversation is often more focused, relevant, and impactful. Structure matters in onboarding.

This example of a focused shadowing system gets us started with onboarding, but even a program for shadowing executives doesn't entirely build the interaction required to foster shared intention. An onboarding program which builds relationships and appreciates employee contributions requires something more: joint work projects with key employees.

Beyond Shadowing

The core of onboarding, of building relationships, is consequential interaction of varying duration with different people. Setting up your onboarding system to ensure integration of your incoming workforce without disrupting business is important, but the risk is your business processes become so focused on training that executing business outcomes suffers. No matter how your system focuses on training and integration, any time training clashes with business output, business output should always take priority.

As a starting point, we'll begin by structuring the work processes of entry-level personnel along group size. It is a matter of structure and opportunity which begins with executives and supervisors continuing to refine their understanding of what the work is, and how it is most effectively accomplished. Starting with your deep understanding of the work to be done by your business model, it's a matter of strategic processing to structure the work into the group sizes detailed as follows:

Individual projects are an opportunity for the employee to have a high level of control, to be creative, and to feel what it's like to have complete responsibility for the decisions and outcomes. This also fosters a consequential ongoing interaction between the new hire and their immediate supervisor. As the supervisor monitors progress, sets deadlines, and nurtures development, the employee will have the chance to demonstrate accountability, initiative, and willingness to accept direction. This fosters improvement in both the employee and the supervisor.

Small team (2–3 people) projects have a unique level of complexity. They are simpler than larger groups because fewer personalities are at play, but personality conflict is much more difficult to avoid when fewer people are in the room. If the personalities get along, the challenge will be to ensure a high level of quality is reached. When small groups agree, often they agree that "good enough" is good enough. The supervisor will have the challenge of ensuring performance standards are met with a group that may not be inclined to agree. More difficult, if the individuals in a small group clash, the challenge will be figuring out how to work together and produce the outcome notwithstanding the negative emotion. The key here is for the supervisor to engage in high-level coaching for the individuals and then ensure they figure out how to get past the personality conflict and focus on the outcome. Again, this fosters improvement for both the small group and the supervisor.

Medium (4–9 people)-sized teams are the next step and can be used as a test bed for a more senior new employee, someone who may be nearing the end of the onboarding cycle. Giving this person a team leader role where they use what they have learned in the onboarding program to bring a larger group together to produce an outcome is useful in leadership assessment and provides the team leader with the next phase of accomplishment and learning. New employees will be able to experience the freedom of movement that comes from a larger team. Personality conflicts are easier to avoid, but team interaction is still necessary. In addition, while working in smaller teams requires all personality disputes to be addressed, a medium-sized team presents the option of avoiding the conflict by separating the personnel who are having difficulty getting along. This is a choice not found in smaller teams, but is one which must be applied sparingly and usually only for reasons related to time frame.

Nothing is really solved by separating combatants, but if the project will be completed in four days, it may be the best option to get the work done on time. The point is to recognize medium-sized groups present unique choices regarding whether to take the time required to work through difficult interactions (required in the small group) with avoidance of problem interactions through separation of personnel (easier and more effective in large groups). Avoidance, when judiciously used to meet a deadline, can be effective; but it is never an effective solution to the problem (it just meets the deadline). This lesson is unique to the medium-sized group. This also gives the supervisor the opportunity to observe and coach an emerging leader—yet another type of development.

Large (10+ people) groups are necessarily messier and should most often be led by the supervisor. The challenge here is to ensure the new employees (and some of the old ones) don't hide in the larger group and avoid contributing at all. The large group actually closes the loop with the individual project in that it provides the opportunity for individuals and small groups to demonstrate initiative and team building within the greater project.

Consequential projects: Moving new employees through an array of different sized work teams and different work partners is important, but only insofar as it develops the employees' ability to foster work relationships with a broad array of individuals. This system will also reveal to supervisors who is capable in what specialties and who works best together in various circumstances. Having these data then allows supervisors and executives to assemble the best available team to work on consequential projects—the projects which are high risk, high visibility, or time sensitive. The entire team system reveals what you need to know to build the A-teams you need when you need them.

So, how does the rest of this work?

Structure and Execution

The final component of building an effective onboarding program is to understand onboarding is not linear, and work assignments should not be linear either. There should be no set progression where, for example, a new person starts with an individual project, once successful rises to a small group, and so on. Nor should a new hire be immediately assigned to a large team where the choice is "keep your head down and pay your dues" or struggle to contribute. On the contrary, each new employee should be initially assessed by the supervisor or the supervisory team and assigned to either two or three different sized teams with different projects based on what the assessment reveals to be their strengths.

This is not as difficult as it sounds, because you've actually already done the assessment during the behavioral interview. We've already mentioned that part of a recommendation to hire, regardless of whether a candidate is Successful or Failure–Coachable, is the first draft of the onboarding plan. Well, here we are—onboarding. A strong self-starter might be given an individual project and a large group project, with possibly a medium project, should one be available. Another new employee, one who has excellent interpersonal and personality assessment skills, might be assigned to both a small and a medium team, and possibly to a large team if one is available. By working simultaneously on several projects, which require different types of interpersonal interaction skills, more will be revealed about the employee, and the employee will experience faster and more functional development.

The point is to recognize onboarding is not one-size-fits-all training. It is structured, consequential interaction with a variety of people across the organization. And the projects do not need to all be cybersecurity projects. Part of the process should be for supervisors and team leaders to understand the business well enough that they can make reasonable recommendations for assigning apprentice and journeyman level cybersecurity personnel to teams working on projects which are not necessarily cybersecurity projects. By working on consequential projects across business lines in groups of varying size, more employees will be able to put a face to cybersecurity, and your cybersecurity personnel will understand how the business functions. In addition to integrating new employees into the corporate culture efficiently through relationships, this system also causes continued improvement across the business—and that's the point. Amanda Tilly describes it this way:

> **Amanda:** We have worked to create relationships with all departments in our organization. We've experienced incidents, and

we know we're being successful when people know who to call right away. They know who we are; they may not understand the technology behind it, they may not understand every little intricate detail of information security, but they know who we are, and they know how to reach us, and that's how we know we're being effective.[12]

This system of team projects drives those relationships. Building an environment which fosters the ongoing need to create relationships drives a deeper understanding of people across your organization. And not just an "executive level" of understanding where only supervisors have a deep understanding of individual contributors, but rather an environment where everyone participates in an ongoing interaction which fosters understanding of each other. Andrea Markstrom explains her process in keeping the team together:

> **Andrea:** Instead of me being directive and expecting my team to be order-takers, I shift that and turn to them for ideas, recommendations, solutions. They are empowered, they are part of the discussion. I look to them. I mean, that's the talent right there. I am merely the connector. It is my team who is the braintrust, and if they're not with me or part of that discussion, then it's not going to go anywhere. The other piece I've spent a lot of time sharing with my team is that the world of IT is changing; more and more of what we do is shifting to the cloud, or a managed service provider, so I explain to my team across the board in IT that every role is changing. I want their input as to how we can change it together so that they feel a part of that, and they're invested in it, but also so that they understand the why and create and share the vision. We, as leaders, need to set the stage and then let the team shine.[13]

All of what Andrea describes about her "braintrust" contributes toward creating a sense of belonging, recognizes the value of each team member's

---

[12] A. Tilley, in discussion with the authors. July 02, 2020.
[13] A. Markstrom, in discussion with the authors. June 24, 2020.

contribution, and fosters shared intention, in front of the rapidly changing world of IT. T.J. Harrington offers another perspective regarding how leadership should function to cultivate the team:

> **T.J.:** When driving crisis management, it is important to lead by example. One of the first things I had to deal with was Hurricane Sandy when I arrived at Citi. I show up, and within a few weeks we've got the hurricane. I was in that command post virtually for three days—going to a hotel to catch a little bit of shut eye, with a third of Manhattan in the dark. The crisis management people who worked for me said afterwards that they couldn't believe the boss was there. They'd never seen that, and some of them had worked for the bank for twenty-plus years. They were so used to the executive just coming in and checking in and checking out, as opposed to being there, being available, listening to the issues and challenges, asking questions and being concerned about the folks.[14]

This leads us to a few final thoughts on employee onboarding and employee development. Planning for turnover focuses on Failure–Coachable and has two positive impacts on your organization. First, it gives entry-level opportunity to the right people at low risk to you and them. If a new employee doesn't work out, terminating them won't disrupt a system which anticipates employees will move on in a year or two anyway. It also minimizes the risk to the candidate. They can have a try at working in your system, and if it doesn't suit them, they can move on without damage to their career.

Second, it creates an always-learning/always-training environment in your company. Since you will likely have a steady stream of new people coming on board, you'll have a steady need for training. Since training is a perishable skill and training needs to be revised and updated to stay current, constant training facilitates practice and improvement. It also fosters an apprentice system. Your journeymen and journeywomen, those who

---

[14] T.J. Harrington, in discussion with the authors. July 31, 2020.

have gone through the initial two years and moved on to the next job, are best positioned to coach the new entries. They are also ready to begin coaching and teaching—a key process in their own development. The old military system works well here. To really learn a skill: "watch one, do one, teach one." Having these employees as a key part of your entry-level employee onboarding not only streamlines the process of integrating new employees into your business but also enhances their skills right when they need the challenge. By developing partnerships with both the training programs which feed people into entry-level jobs and the mid-level hiring managers who see entry-level employees as their hiring pool, you'll have a strong and flexible system capable of withstanding the ebb and flow of entry-level employees across your company. Blocking the flow and creating a static system creates the need for a large and cumbersome HR system, while also not solving a high turnover problem.

Incorporating Cybersecurity Into All Employee Onboarding

Tangentially related to onboarding new cybersecurity hires is the subject of cybersecurity awareness being baked into all employee onboarding. That's right: not only are we arguing that most companies and government agencies need to hire cyber talent, but all employees need to be made aware and trained on cybersecurity issues! As of early 2020, nearly a quarter of data breaches in the United States were caused by human error.[15] Globally, cybersecurity employee training can shave about $238,000 off the average total $3.86M cost of a data breach.[16] And according to a recent SANS survey, among those organizations whose leadership believes their peer organizations are investing significantly in security awareness training, 69 percent of them are treating the issue as a top priority.[17] This

---

[15] Ponemon, *Cost of a Data Breach Report 2020*. www.ibm.com/security/digital-assets/cost-data-breach-report/#/pdf (33)

[16] *Id.* at 42.

[17] SANS. 2019. "SANS Security Awareness Report: The Rising Era of Awareness Training." www.sans.org/security-awareness-training/reports/2019-security-awareness-report (4)

number continues to rise, but all organizations must understand the importance of cybersecurity awareness training in order to help combat security threats from all sides.

Cybersecurity awareness training programs can take many forms. Such programs may be custom created by your in-house cybersecurity team, purchased from and run by a commercial vendor, or a combination. Amanda explains information security is addressed during new hire training, and beyond, at her financial institution employer:

> **Amanda:** In our organization, cybersecurity education starts at new hire training with a presentation which is followed by an online new hire information security training. We also conduct regular touchpoints with each department. We have worked to create relationships with all departments in our organization. We know information security is becoming top-of-mind to our business lines as they communicate more frequently about suspicious activity, have a better understanding as to why certain controls are in place, and ultimately, that they know who to call in a potential incident. They know who we are, they may not understand the technology behind it, they may not understand every little intricate detail of information security, but they know how to reach us, and that's how we know we're being effective.[18]

This approach—placing cybersecurity awareness in the initial new hire training presentations—is a great way to set the tone for the importance of security in a digitized setting. The "regular touchpoints" Amanda also mentions are vital—building out cybersecurity training with repeated interactions reinforces the fact that cybersecurity requires attention and diligence. Much of this relates back to the idea discussed in multiple chapters of this book, to create and maintain a culture of cybersecurity.

Inherent in creating and sustaining a culture of cybersecurity is incentivizing behaviors you want. While you've now sought out certain *Can* and *Will* particulars for certain cybersecurity jobs, the entirety of the business

---

[18] A. Tilley, in discussion with the authors. July 02, 2020.

does not possess the same foundation. For example: in general society, it is considered rude to not hold the door for the next person coming into the building, or a room. However, for physical and cybersecurity purposes, holding the door poses a threat. The goal for a secure building is to monitor who is going in and out, in no uncertain terms. How do you change the paradigm? How do you incentivize behaviors you want?

Most companies go straight to compliance. They promulgate a rule which prohibits holding the door and requires each individual to badge in and out. The rule is immediately followed by enforcement systems. Guards are stationed, cameras are installed and monitored, and infractions recorded. The problem with a compliance system is that it's an external strategy. The "company" has a rule, and "employees" must comply. There is a better way. The reason for the rule, regardless of what the actual rule might be, is to keep the company from being harmed. Whether it's complying with government regulation so the company doesn't get shut down, or preventing theft, the rule is always about protecting the company. All that remains is fostering a sense of ownership in the company, so each individual wants to protect it, because they feel like it belongs to them. Is this easy? No. Again, it's not a one-size-fits-all process—but it works. As Adam Lee explains, cybersecurity requires "constant engagement," and the entire company needs to buy-in:

> **Adam:** It also takes constant engagement. Training, awareness, and driving awareness to the WHY. You can do a lot simply by saying, "because we said so." You can get to maybe a six out of ten in cyber just forcing it into place with enforced policies. But the final forty percent takes support and buy-in from the company and its workforce. They have to know WHY phishing is a threat … WHY they can't just p-card a new cyber system and plug it in … WHY they can't just install anything they want … WHY they need to report odd things for investigation, etc. The WHY is very powerful in corporate cyber security if you tell the right story and you resolve "what's in it for me?"[19]

---

[19] A. Lee, in discussion with the authors. July 09, 2020.

Correlating Adam's "WHY" with cybersecurity onboarding procedure should reference the organization's mission statement. Proactive cybersecurity training helps protect the whole of the business, and allows the business to fulfill its mission statement. Establishing cybersecurity awareness training as part of the onboarding process sets the stage for acceptance of cybersecurity as a fundamental element of working at your organization. Every employee, no matter what division or level of seniority, is the front line of defense in cyberspace. It can be as simple as reinforcing the basics of cyber hygiene (passwords, phishing vigilance, the principle of least privilege) and as complex as the specifics of your industry (for chemical plants, process control; for financial institutions, supply chain compliance). Every employee plays a part in the cybersecurity of an entire organization. Whether errors are made innocently (by accidently clicking on a phishing e-mail) or maliciously (through a true insider threat), the human element of cybersecurity requires attention.

CHAPTER 8

Concluding Thoughts and Tips for Candidates

Reflecting on the lessons of this cybersecurity workforce development process, it's important to get back to basics. This book intends to lead you through a complex jungle by taking the first deep cut at the trail. The *Can–Trust–Will* path will take you from start to finish, as long as you follow the key markers. First, ensure you understand what you actually need on your cybersecurity team. Knowing the basics of the field of cybersecurity and how it interacts with your organization is the starting point. Second, get the job description down to brass tacks: the *Can* and the *Will* of the job role. Next, build your preliminary candidate pool wisely: use your network to learn who is out there, use recruiters as partners, use conferences as knowledge builders and candidate showcases, and re-learn the purpose and significance of the resumé.

Candidates choosing to be proactive and read this book: kudos. The detailed background of the *Can–Trust–Will* hiring process, in addition to the insights of leaders in the cybersecurity field, offers unparalleled access on how to be the best candidate for the right job role for you. In addition to the lessons and observations of the book, remember to hone in on why you love this field. What knowledge do you have about it? Where did you learn it? What behaviors do you have that make you a fit for certain cybersecurity roles?

Rodney Petersen explains the significance of career awareness in the field of cybersecurity, and why people interested in learning more about, starting, or transitioning to a career in cybersecurity should know there are multiple pathways in:

> **Rodney:** An important element of the strategy related to the cybersecurity workforce is what it means to work in a cybersecurity-

related career. Increasing career discovery, career awareness, is another area that we are focusing on with a dedicated week on career awareness. While that is a good start, I think we'll do more over time. Learning and credentialing systems continue to evolve, and there is recognition that academic degrees are just one pathway to a role in cybersecurity. So are apprenticeships, so are career changes for individuals who have relevant life experiences or work experiences. As a community we can help people to think broadly about the multiple pathways to a career in cybersecurity. I think those are some of the general trends that we're seeing over the coming year.[1]

Can you solve the problems being faced by your prospective employer? Can you do what they need done? Can you fix the things they have broken? Can you work in a team? Can you speak "people" and not just "tech"? Are you committed to "right" instead of "no"? How much does what Nick Davis has to say resonate with you?

Nick: You really need people who love the subject area who care about themselves, because you can't be sitting around babysitting people in information security. You need those people to take the responsibility you give them. Otherwise they're not going to be interested, they're not going to be adaptive, and you're not going to get done what you need to get done.[2]

Regarding how you get to the proper knowledge base, it is becoming clearer that if you have the skill, then not having degrees and certifications is less and less likely to be a barrier to entry. We, alongside our contributors, are not saying to ignore the typical degree process; working toward and obtaining a degree can demonstrate determination, passion, and skill. What we are saying is that businesses—employers—are now seeing that degrees don't necessarily correlate to success in cybersecurity. What does that mean for you as an employee? It means an employer with a degree prerequisite probably has a bureaucratic culture which fails to recognize

---

[1] R. Petersen, in discussion with the authors.
[2] N. Davis, in discussion with the authors. July 27, 2020.

when changes need to be made. This is not the only thing to consider when deciding whether to accept employment, but it should be a part of your decision-making process if they make you a job offer.

The innate curiosity, the need to learn, the desire for the difficult problem, figuring things out rather than needing to be right is much more relevant than degrees and certifications. Consequently, this is the mindset the best employers look for in hiring.

Here are a few bullet points which most of our industry experts repeated:

- Learn to search for what you don't know and what you can't solve. When you get there, learn to find others who, when working together, can quickly and correctly get to "right."
- Be a learner, be an unafraid problem solver. Get comfortable with being uncomfortable.
- It's the accomplishment, not the spotlight which matters. Learn to make the accomplishment of someone on your team a source of visceral satisfaction for you.
- Cybersecurity is a career for a naturally curious person who is also a fast learner.
- Communication is key. If you can't communicate, you'll struggle to land a job and you'll struggle in the job you get.
- Know network architecture and general system structure.
- Don't be afraid to break things and want to learn how to fix them.
- The stereotypical tech "answer guy" is now a fail.
- Desire to be a member of a team and everything being on a team means.

A great statement of the core concept comes from The New Zealand All Blacks rugby team. They have fifteen Principles for Success which the team lives by. Principle number six is simple and impactful and applies here:

Principle No. 6: No Dickheads. Excuse the language but it conveys the point. You want to enhance your team by adding talented players but that doesn't mean that any talented player will do.

The All Blacks are very much a team first and look to find individuals who have the right character. You can develop talent, you cannot change character.[3]

It is said there are many extraordinarily talented rugby players in New Zealand who will never pull an All Blacks jersey over their heads—simply because they do not have the character required to put themselves second and the team first. Every single one of the cybersecurity industry experts we interviewed for this book raised and articulated this principle in their own way—every single one.

Finally, ensure you work to create and grow relationships within your company and within your network. As Andrea Markstrom explains:

Andrea: The most important and valuable step that helped me the most was forming relationships right from the get go. For example, at Target, I was a level-one voice engineer, the CIO at the time was a woman. I aspired to be in that role someday and thought she did an amazing job. I observed how she conducts herself and manages herself, and I just went out on a limb and invited her to a meeting to see if I could learn from her. She accepted and provided invaluable advice and insight. It's about extending yourself and asking for not only to learn from people but asking for help. Ask leaders that inspire you if they would be willing to be a mentor advisor for you. Those relationships are treasures. Don't forget to give back and be a mentor and advisor to others. That is an incredible learning experience as well. I've done this throughout my career, so important and so valuable.[4]

This type of guiding relationship—mentor or less formal—is truly invaluable. Amanda Tilley outlines how mentors have helped her uncover the fields of information security and cybersecurity:

[3] 15 All Black Principles. https://thewhitehorsefederation.org.uk/downloads/default/All-blacks-Poster_01.pdf

[4] A. Markstrom, in discussion with the authors. June 24, 2020.

Amanda: I never thought I'd be working in information security. I didn't have a technical degree, I didn't know many women pursuing cybersecurity, and I didn't know that information security was so much more than hackers in hoodies. I've been incredibly fortunate over the years to have mentors in my workplace who actively challenge me to shape and achieve my potential. I cannot stress enough how important that cross-departmental mentorship is for career development. Perhaps that analyst in accounting or risk management with a political science degree could be your team's next leader in information security?[5]

Circling back, if you are transitioning to a career in cybersecurity, or are coming from a noncomputer science background, cybersecurity may still be for you. Many of the new entries to the cybersecurity workforce come from nontechnical backgrounds, as Amanda points out. And generally, the opportunities in cybersecurity are diverse, expanding, and constantly evolving.

The following appendices are not intended to be a resource from which you can cut and paste. Rather, they are intended as a starting point, an example of how to articulate behavioral characteristics. Part of an effective behavioral interview is ensuring it's correctly (and custom!) built, and drafting your own description of the terms you use is an integral part of the thought process. You may note that some of the questions we outline seem close to being duplicates, and some of the characteristics we highlight may overlap to a large degree. This underscores the concept that there is no magic question, nor is there a correct answer. Alternative formulations aid in digging down to the stories which reveal whether a candidate has the behavioral characteristics you need. And that's the goal—to understand.

The point of these appendices is to trigger your thinking, not give you answers. You simply can't build or conduct a behavioral interview without thinking deeply about it. We offer the following as a diving board; jump in with your own roles and responsibilities and identify the behaviors which correlate to success in each job at your company.

---

[5] A. Tilley, in discussion with the authors. July 02, 2020.

Appendix A

Model Behavioral Question Sets

CISO (Executive)

- Calm under fire.
  - Tell us about a time when you had to make a choice that affected someone close to you, but you didn't have enough information to be confident in your decision. What did you do?
  - Tell us about a time when you had to make a decision without having enough time to fully consider the alternatives. What was the outcome and how did you deal with the outcome?
  - Tell us about a time when a crucial piece of equipment failed on you (car, photocopier, air conditioner, computer). What did you do? How did you interact with others in the situation? How was the situation resolved?
- Organized multitasker.
  - Tell us about your biggest time crunch; a situation where you had significantly more things to do than you had time to do them in. How did you decide what to do and how did you deal with the consequences?
  - Tell us about a time when you were given a large assignment with no lead time and a short deadline. How did you cope? What was the outcome?
- Communicates opinions with ease.
  - Tell us about a time when you had to give bad news to someone close to you.
  - Tell us about a time when you disagreed with someone close to you about something important. How did you tell them?

- ○ Tell us about a time when you disagreed with someone you disliked about something important. How did you tell them?
- Ability to clearly direct people.
  - ○ Tell us about a time when you had to give instructions for an immediate task to someone who was struggling to understand.
  - ○ Tell us about a time when you had to assign a project to someone you didn't like and whom you felt was incapable of accomplishing the task. What did you do?
  - ○ Tell us about a time when you assigned a complex task to a large group. How did you ensure everyone knew what to do?
- Solid decision-making skills.
  - ○ Tell us about a time when you made a decision which was initially seen as disastrous, but eventually turned out to be correct.
  - ○ Tell us about a time when you had to make a controversial decision which impacted people close to you. How did you go about making the decision and communicating it to those who needed to know? What happened? How did you implement the decision?

Network Engineer (Mid–Senior Level)

- Quick reflexes.
  - ○ Tell us about the quickest decision you ever made.
  - ○ Tell us about a snap decision you made where you got it wrong. Tell us about the next decision you faced.
  - ○ Tell us about a time when you faced a series of snap decisions where each choice impacted the next decision and where you didn't have time to stop and think. How did you cope?
- Passionate about subject area.
  - ○ Tell us about a time when you realized your excitement about a topic caused you to monopolize a conversation and annoy the other participants? How did you respond?

- ° Tell us about a time when you were assigned a task for which you had no enthusiasm. How did it impact your performance? How did you cope?
- Reviews information and situations critically.
  - ° Tell us about a time when you had to review the performance of someone close to you. How did you ensure your review was unbiased by your preexisting feelings toward that person?
  - ° Tell us about a time when you shared your honest assessment with someone who had asked for your opinion but was actually just looking for approval. What did you do?
  - ° Have you ever been in a "the emperor has no clothes" situation? What did you do?
- Does not have to be major "team player" or very socially capable, but able to communicate across teams.
  - ° Tell us about a time when you had to communicate something important to a person you either didn't like or didn't know very well. How did you ensure they understood your message?
  - ° Tell us about a time when you quickly built rapport with a person you didn't know.
  - ° Tell us about a time when you exchanged consequential information with someone you did not know very well. How did you quickly build trust? How confident were you in the level of communication when the exchange was completed?
- Attention to detail.
  - ° Tell us about a time when you saw issues or problems which everyone else appeared to either not see or not be concerned about. What did you do? How did you cope?
  - ° Tell us about a time when you were criticized for being "too in the weeds." How did you respond? What did you do to resolve the issue?
  - ° Tell us about a time when your preparation process for a project took far longer than the time allowed. How did you cope?

- Problem-solver mentality.
  - Tell us about a time when people important to you were in conflict. What did you do? How did you cope? What was the outcome?
  - Tell us about a time you were presented with a problem you thought you couldn't solve. What did you do?
- Time management.
  - Tell us about a time when someone important to you needed more of your time than you could give them. What did you do to resolve the issue?
  - Tell us about a time when you were late.
  - Tell us about a time when you were interrupted and pulled away from something important. How did you cope?

Incident Responder (Senior Level)

- Quick reflexes.
  - Tell us about the quickest decision you ever made.
  - Tell us about a snap decision you made where you got it wrong. Tell us about the next decision you faced.
  - Tell us about a time when you faced a series of snap decisions where each choice impacted the next decision and where you didn't have time to stop and think. How did you cope?
- Good communicator.
  - Tell us about a time you had difficulty communicating with someone important to you. How did you cope? What strategies did you use to reconnect?
  - Tell us about a time when you had an important message to deliver which you expected would be rejected, misunderstood, or otherwise not well-received. What did you do?
  - Tell us about your most recent public speaking engagement.
- Reviews information and situations critically.
  - Tell us about a time when you had to review the performance of someone close to you. How did you ensure your

review was unbiased by your preexisting feelings toward that person?

- ○ Tell us about a time when you shared your honest assessment with someone who had asked for your opinion but was actually just looking for approval. What did you do?
- ○ Have you ever been in a "the emperor has no clothes" situation? What did you do?

- Can handle pressure well.
  - ○ Tell us about one of your most stressful experiences. How did you handle it? How did you cope?
  - ○ Tell us about a time when you were required to do something you found to be extremely unpleasant. How did you cope?
  - ○ Tell us about a time you struggled to get through the learning curve of a new job or project. How did you handle the situation? What was the outcome?

- Can act without emotion in stressful situations.
  - ○ Tell us about a time when someone close to you did something wrong or unethical. How did you respond?
  - ○ Tell us about a time when you made a mistake that really mattered. What did you do going forward?
  - ○ Tell us about a time when you didn't get something you were entitled to. How did you feel? What did you do to handle the situation?

- Thorough.
  - ○ Tell us about a time when other team members thought a project was completed but you thought there was much more work to do. What did you do to resolve the disagreement?
  - ○ Tell us about a time when you were on a team with someone who always did the bare minimum. How did you cope? What did you do?

- Attention to detail.
  - ○ Tell us about a time when you saw issues or problems which everyone else appeared to either not see or not be concerned about. What did you do? How did you cope?

- Tell us about a time when you were criticized for being "too in the weeds." How did you respond? What did you do to resolve the issue?
- Tell us about a time when your preparation process for a project took far longer than the time allowed. How did you cope?

- Able to jump start.
  - Tell us about a time you set a goal that nobody thought you could achieve. How did you handle the situation? What was the outcome?
  - Tell us about a time when you did more than was required on your own initiative. Specifically, how did you come to decide to do more, how did you decide what to do, and how did you deal with acting without permission?

Systems Administrator (Entry Level)

A. Social skills.
  - (a) Tell us about a time you were on a team with people you didn't get along with. How did you cope? What was the outcome?
  - (b) Tell us about a time when you stood up for someone or something when doing so was unpopular.
  - (c) Tell us about a time when you intervened to prevent a bad outcome.
B. Thorough researcher.
  - (a) Tell us about a research project when you did more than was required on your own initiative. Specifically, how did you come to decide to do more and how did you decide how far to go?
  - (b) Tell us about a research project where you followed every alternative theory to its logical conclusion. How did you balance the use of additional time and resources against the marginal gain?
C. Able to take direction with ease.
  - (a) Tell us about a time when you had difficulty adjusting to a new role at work or at school. What did you do? How did you cope?
  - (b) Tell us about a time when a person in authority (a parent, a boss, a teacher) directed you to do something you thought was a waste

of time. What did you do? How did you resolve your internal conflict?

D. Able to take criticism without sensitivity.

    (a) Tell us about a time you disagreed with someone in authority (a parent, a boss, a teacher) about something important. What did you do? How did you cope? What was the outcome?

    (b) Tell us about a time when someone you dislike gave you bad news? How did you react? How did you cope?

E. Good communicator.

    (a) Tell us about a time you had difficulty communicating with someone important to you. How did you cope? What strategies did you use to reconnect?

    (b) Tell us about a time when you had an important message to deliver which you expected would be rejected, misunderstood, or otherwise not well-received. What did you do?

    (c) Tell us about the last time you spoke to a large audience.

Appendix B

Additional Behavioral Question Sets

Inquisitiveness

- Tell us about a time when you did something everyone thought was foolish just to find out what it was like.
- What was the last puzzle that kept you up all night?
- Tell us about the last thing you designed.
- Tell us about the puzzle that took you the longest to solve.

Curiosity

- Tell us about a time you fixed something that everyone else thought was beyond repair.
- Tell us about a time when you took something apart and weren't able to put it back together.
- Tell us about a time when you stepped back from a problem and let it go.
- What's the most difficult puzzle you ever solved?

Fast Learner

- Tell us about a time when you didn't understand a set of directions.
- Tell us about a time when you had to figure out how to fix something before the return of an authority figure (parent, teacher, boss).

Procedure, Detail, and Repetition

- Tell us about the last time you had to follow a precise set of instructions. A recipe or assembly of some sort.
- Tell us about a time when you had a strong emotional reaction to doing the same thing twice.
- Tell us about a time when you had to do a specific task without any direction other than to produce the outcome.
- Tell us about a time when you were given a precise set of instructions and as you worked through them, you discovered that they were wrong.

Commitment to Company

- Tell us about a time when you were required to enforce a rule with which you disagreed.
- Tell us about a time when your boss made a judgment call with which you disagreed.

Shared Intention

- Tell us about the best team you were ever on. What made it great?
- Tell us about the most difficult thing you ever did that relied on someone else to contribute to the outcome.
- Tell us about a time where you willingly share credit for a significant accomplishment with someone else.

Mission Before Self

- Tell us about a time you needed to apologize to someone.
- Tell us about a time when you did what someone else needed instead of what you wanted.
- Tell us about a time when you thought you had an important role but you were not treated as a key member of the team.

Ability to Be Client-Facing

- Tell us about a time when you had to execute someone else's plan.
- Tell us about a project you did where you weren't a part of making the decisions.
- Tell us about the most difficult time you have had communicating with someone.
- Tell us about a time when you built something that someone else designed.

Moral Compass

- Tell us about a time when you had made a commitment and then were faced with a new circumstance which made it difficult to keep the commitment. How did you balance the competing interests? What did you do?
- Tell us about a time when you began executing your plan B and then plan A materialized. What did you do?
- Tell us about a situation where an authority figure (parent, teacher, boss) wanted you to do something you thought was wrong. How did you respond? What did you do? How was the situation resolved?
- Tell us about a time when you had the ability to harm someone's reputation.

About the Authors

Leeza Garber, Esq. is a consultant and attorney, specializing in cyber-security and privacy law. Leeza is an award-winning lecturer at The Wharton School, University of Pennsylvania, teaching Internet Law, Privacy, and Cybersecurity, and is also an adjunct law professor at Drexel University's Kline School of Law, focused on information privacy. She appears as an on-air analyst on Fox News Channel, Fox Business Network, The National Desk and others, providing expert insight on cybersecurity, privacy, social media, and technology-related news. Leeza has been published in *The Hill, Wired, The Legal Intelligencer* and *Newsweek*. She presents as a keynote speaker for legal and technology conferences and corporate events nationwide. Leeza previously worked as in-house counsel for a cybersecurity and digital forensics company. Leeza graduated from the University of Pennsylvania Law School with a certificate in business and public policy from The Wharton School, University of Pennsylvania, and earned her BA cum laude from Bryn Mawr College.

Scott Olson is the CEO of Olson Strategic Initiatives and Founder of GlenHaven International, LLC. During a twenty-seven-year career in government, Scott served as a Deputy Prosecuting Attorney and an FBI Special Agent where he was a counterintelligence operations officer, an Assistant Special Agent in Charge of Intelligence and Counterintelligence, and the FBI's Legal Attaché in Baghdad, Iraq. Scott also developed and implemented the FBI's Leadership Development Program and one of the FBI's senior executive leadership assessment processes. As an accomplished Security and HR executive, Scott has extensive experience in all aspects of global security operations and deep expertise in related critical HR processes with an emphasis on leading-edge hiring processes and emerging leader development. Scott is an FBI-certified Interview and Interrogation Instructor and holds a BA in History from the University of Washington and a JD from the Seattle University School of Law.

Leeza and Scott are the co-founders of Can. Trust. Will., LLC, offering consulting services related to their revolutionary, proprietary process that recognizes the human element of hiring. Their work focuses on implementing bespoke workforce development procedures to lead to team success.

Index

ability, 11, 14, 29, 33, 48, 65, 94, 108, 120, 125, 141, 145, 149, 168, 184, 193

Apache Struts, xv

As A Service (AAS), 12–13

Avenson, J., 101–102, 120–121

ball-handling skill, 90

behavioral characteristics, 93–100, 112–114

behavioral interviews, 25, 26, 28, 29, 40, 50–53, 94, 95, 102, 105, 108, 110, 111, 117–119, 125, 127, 128, 131–134, 136–143, 145–154, 169, 181

"belonging to a fraternity," 148

Bender, B., 10–11, 50, 76

Berglas, A., 66, 70–71, 118–119, 131–132

Big Mistake, 26, 60, 82, 85, 88, 95, 97–98, 111, 138, 142, 148, 150, 153

binary assessment, 30

Brennan, B., 36–37, 62, 96, 116, 119–120

Bricker, A., 69, 89, 100–101, 115, 135, 146, 159, 160

budget process, 13–23

buzzwords, 41, 64, 81

Can–Trust–Will, 25–30, 38–42, 54, 82, 83, 99, 107, 108, 116–117, 119, 131–132, 148, 157, 177

career, 33, 67, 69, 70, 75, 77, 106, 171, 177, 178, 181

Carolina Cyber Center, 69

Casale, P., 61, 70, 81, 108

Category-Based Presumptions, 93

certifications, 63–66, 70–73, 95, 107, 178, 179

Chief Information Security Officer (CISO), 6, 11, 112–113, 115, 183–184

Chudolij, M., 35–36, 105–106, 149, 157

CIO/CSO structure, xv–xvi, 88–89, 123, 124

coachable and noncoachable, 31–38

Coleman, W., 52–53, 58, 102–103, 118, 155

commitment, 161, 192, 193

communication, 9, 34, 51, 74, 79, 92, 94, 98, 152, 179, 185

competency, 26, 64–65

consequential projects, 164, 168, 169

Consumer Privacy Act (CCPA), 4

COVID-19, xvii, xviii

creativity, 50, 69, 164

C-Suite, xvi, 1, 18

curiosity, 101, 191

custom program, 7

cyber roles, 116

cybersecurity
    awareness, 172, 173, 175
    culture, xvi–xx
    hiring, 1–2, 91, 126
    job roles, 96–97
    leadership, 58, 59
    obligations, 4–8
    professional development program, 69
    professionals, 119
    risk, budgeting for, 13–23
    roles, 8–13, 105
    standards, 7
    training, 34, 73, 173, 175

Cybersecurity Maturity Model Certification Model Version 1.0 (CMMC), 6–7

Cybersecurity Operations Center, 102

CyberSeek, 61

data aggregators, 45–49
data breach, 5, 121–125, 127, 128, 134, 172
Davis, N., 37–38, 59, 67, 68, 178
decision-making process, 13, 135, 146, 179, 184
developing question, 136–137
diversity, 82, 83, 86, 88, 106, 132, 133
due diligence, 27, 42–49, 85
Durst, M., 41, 148–149

Equifax, xv–xvi, 88
ethics, 125–129

Failure–Coachable, 30–35, 37, 38, 117, 142, 151, 152, 171
Failure-Noncoachable, 30–35, 37, 38, 117, 142, 151, 152
fast learner, 191

General Data Protection Regulation (GDPR), 4
generic personality assessments, 133
Gibson, S., 15, 74–75
"good people" process, 89
"gotcha," 141–147
Gottehrer, G., xix, 1–2, 4, 88, 98–99, 154
gray zone, 154

Harrington, T. J., 23, 124–125, 160–162, 171
hiring, 1, 26, 35, 38, 39, 41, 42, 46, 48–50, 52–54, 65, 72, 77, 79, 82–86, 91, 93–94, 96, 112, 119, 126, 133, 135, 147–149, 153–155, 157, 158
Hornbein, T., 69
human behavior, 90–93
human element, 159, 160, 175, 196
human resource (HR), 9, 32, 39, 58, 63, 79–81, 145, 153, 160, 172, 195

ideal candidate, 63
incident responder, 113–114, 186–188

individual contributors, 65
individual projects, 167
industry standard, 63
information technology (IT), 11, 15, 16, 43, 60, 75, 76, 103, 105, 107, 110, 118, 123, 134, 170
inquisitiveness, 191
interview, 131–133, 136, 153
    analysis, 150–152
    introduction to, 137–139
    process, 139–150
    questions, 133–137
    summary, 152–156
    See also behavioral interviews

job
    description, 27, 29, 39, 54, 62–79, 85, 87, 90, 95, 100, 101, 108, 121, 145, 147, 177
    high turnover, 77–78
    performance, 35, 39, 53, 82, 83, 85, 87, 96, 116, 133–135, 139, 148, 154
    requirement, 60, 62, 72, 74, 80
    role, 27–29, 39, 40, 47, 52–54, 62, 69, 72, 86, 87, 91, 94–97, 99, 101, 103, 106, 109, 111, 112, 115–118, 131, 133, 137, 141, 143, 144, 150–152, 166, 177
    search, 25
    success, 27, 29, 62, 86, 87, 103, 108, 112, 116, 136, 181

Keegan, B., 78–79
knowledge, skills, and abilities (KSA) tests, 85
Kolb, J., 68, 69, 126, 132–133, 146

large (10+ people) groups, 168
last person who had it, 63
leader development, 65
Lee, A., xvii, 3, 7, 58, 99–100, 106–107, 127, 158, 162, 174, 175
legacy systems, 103–104
lifecycle goals, 106–107
liposuction, 103

Markstrom, A., xviii, 15–17, 57, 71,
    134, 141, 154–155, 158–159,
    164–165, 170–171, 180
Maurer, P., 128–129
medium (4–9 people)-sized teams,
    167
mental models, 135
Meszaros, J., 50–51
MGM Grand shooting, 19–20
Michaels, A., 40, 73–74
mission, 192
mission statements, 158–163
moral compass, 193

narrowing process, 108
National Initiative for Cybersecurity
    Education (NICE)
    Cybersecurity Workforce
    Framework, 8–12, 61, 62, 65,
    94, 145
National Institute of Standards and
    Technology (NIST), 8–9
network engineer, 113, 184–186
New York Department of Financial
    Services, 6
NICE Cybersecurity Workforce
    Framework, 145
NICE Framework, 94

onboarding, 35, 49, 53, 93, 142, 149,
    152, 156, 163–166
    employee, 151, 172–175
    shadowing process, 164–168
    shared intention and mission
        statements, 158–163
    structure and execution, 168–172

Pennsylvania Bar Association, xx
personality, 95–100
Petersen, R., 11–12, 64, 65, 136,
    177–178

recruiter services, 78–79
resumé, 79–83
Return On Investment (ROI), 17,
    21, 22

role descriptors, 105–115

security budget, 17, 18, 20
Security Budget Analytic (SBA) loop,
    21–22
Security Operations Center (SOC),
    14
selection process, 111
self-motivation, 77
shadowing process, 164–168
shared intention, 158–163, 192
small team (2–3 people) projects,
    167
Society for Human Resource
    Management (SHRM), 6
soft skills, 108
Stop Hacks and Improve Electronic
    Data Security (SHIELD)
    Act, 5
systems administrator, 114,
    188–189

talent acquisition, 63
teachability, 97
teamwork, 121–125
technical skills, 112–114
    and behaviors, 115–116
Thornton, B., 80, 92, 107
360-degree perspective, 89
Tilley, A., 5, 18–19, 37, 41–44,
    75–76, 84, 97, 123, 144,
    169–170, 173, 180–181
trust, 42–49, 121–125
23 NYCRR 500: Cybersecurity
    Requirements for Financial
    Services Companies, 6

Uber data breach, 121–125, 127
uncommon characteristics, 100–104
uncovering behaviors, 115–125
U.S. Department of Labor, 116

Woodson, M., 2–3, 9–10, 20, 58,
    66–67, 80, 98, 123–124,
    161–162
"worker bees," 118

OTHER TITLES IN THE BUSINESS LAW AND CORPORATE RISK MANAGEMENT COLLECTION

John Wood, Econautics Sustainability Institute, Editor

- *Business Sustainability* by Zabihollah Rezaee
- *Business Sustainability Factors of Performance, Risk, and Disclosure* by Zabihollah Rezaee
- *The Gig Mafia* by David M. Shapiro
- *Guerrilla Warfare in the Corporate Jungle* by K. F. Dochartaigh
- *A Book About Blockchain* by Rajat Rajbhandari
- *Successful Cybersecurity Professionals* by Steven Brown
- *Artificial Intelligence for Risk Management* by Archie Addo, Srini Centhala, and Muthu Shammugam

Concise and Applied Business Books

The Collection listed above is one of 30 business subject collections that Business Expert Press has grown to make BEP a premiere publisher of print and digital books. Our concise and applied books are for...

- Professionals and Practitioners
- Faculty who adopt our books for courses
- Librarians who know that BEP's Digital Libraries are a unique way to offer students ebooks to download, not restricted with any digital rights management
- Executive Training Course Leaders
- Business Seminar Organizers

Business Expert Press books are for anyone who needs to dig deeper on business ideas, goals, and solutions to everyday problems. Whether one print book, one ebook, or buying a digital library of 110 ebooks, we remain the affordable and smart way to be business smart. For more information, please visit www.businessexpertpress.com, or contact sales@businessexpertpress.com.

CPSIA information can be obtained
at www.ICGtesting.com
Printed in the USA
BVHW091037290122
627446BV00006B/173